HIDDEN A<

BY

PETER BREUER ©

GET A LIFE

HOLLANDER PUBLICATIONS

ENGLAND

First published in Great Britain in 2011 by

Hollander Publications

ISBN   978-0-9570067-0-6

hollanderpublications@hotmail.co.uk

TABLE of CONTENTS

Distant Memories - Meditation in a new light

MEDITATION

Peter Breuer

We drag around, without a doubt,
it's no use to deny it,
some hang-ups we could do without,
if we could only find it.

You have, of course, a perfect mind.
That fact goes without saying.
You have no flaw of any kind:
No ghost which could need laying.

But, then again, it could just be
that you are not quite perfect;
your free will is not truly free,
because of a concealed affect.

A memory you can not bear,
which you once firmly banished,
of which you are not now aware,
by which you would be tarnished.

Think on these things, and ponder well
in quiet meditation,
what memory could make you ill,
or cause you black depression.

Humility must be your guide
to face the truth with valour.
There's really nowhere you can hide.
Your best defence is candour.

It's only pride, which stands between
your troubles and elation.
Face up to what you've done or seen,
and that will bring salvation.

FOREWORD

There are three sorts of health. There is physical health, there is mental health, but by no means least, there is also emotional health. This book is about emotional health, and the way in which it can affect the other two sorts of health.

The importance of emotional health is not always recognised. The Romans spoke of: **mens sana in corpore sano** (*a healthy mind in a healthy body*) as the human ideal. They should have spoken of "A healthy mind in a healthy body, with healthy emotions". The Greeks had a clearer view of the matter. That is why they wrote **"Know Thyself"** on the lintel above the entrance to the temple at Delphi.

Two consequences arise from ignoring emotional health. One is that the symptoms of emotional ill-health are often mistaken for mental ill-health or even mental illness. The other is that those illnesses, which are called psycho-somatic illnesses, as if there were something wrong with the psyche (*mind*) are not recognised as being due to emotional ill-health. That does a lot of harm, because nobody wants to be thought of as mentally ill.

In fact, people with a psycho-somatic illness, who need the treatment called psycho-therapy have perfect (often brilliant) minds. Their problem is emotional constipation.

A SUMMARY OF HIDDEN AGENDAS

This book is called Hidden Agendas. It might equally well be called "Spellbound", "Windmills of the Mind" or "The Mesmer Loop". It could reasonably be called "Beyond the Microscope".

Its aim is to make readers more aware of their subconscious minds, and of the subconscious mind's potential effect on emotional health.
It tells readers that the subconscious mind is capable of holding data about past experiences, and at the same time concealing that data from the conscious mind.
It tells readers that the purpose of that concealment was originally to protect the body from the emotional overload of a distressing experience (real or imaginary)
It tells readers that the nerve impulses from the concealment of the experience produce "side effects" (affects).
It tells readers that the form which that "side effect" actually takes in any one individual is unpredictable
It tells readers that the concealed data can not be brought to light, or its affect overcome, by willpower
It tells readers that nobody can find the concealed data, except the individual's own subconscious mind.
It tells readers that when the data is brought back to light, and the particular emotion, on account of which it was concealed, is discharged, the particular problem (affect) which the concealment caused, is gone.
It tells readers that the previously concealed memory gets incorporated into the individual's wealth of useful experiences.
Finally the book hints (it can do no more than hint) at the infinite number and variety of the blocks and hang-ups technically known as psycho-neuroses. They are best described as emotional constipation.

The effect of psycho-neuroses is felt in all aspects of everyday life, in every form of social interaction, and in the overall health of society.
Politicians, whether of the dictatorial or democratic variety, would be quite different people without their hang-ups. In consequence the effect of psycho-neuroses is a determining factor in politics, and so plays a dramatic roll in the twists and turns of history.

The book mentions, but does not aim to explain, the therapies which can deal with such problems. Until the problem itself is understood, the relevant therapies will not be universally accepted and adopted as a normal rite of passage.

In this book there are about forty-four chapters, five of which are case histories as told by the therapist, under whose guidance the client's own mind found the cause of the client's problem.

CHARCOT

Charcot, a famous neurologist, worked in France in the late nineteenth century. At that time it was thought that one of his patients, a man with very bad St.Vitus Dance, had his nervous system destroyed by a lightening strike, while he was sheltering under a tree during a thunderstorm. All that man's limbs were constantly shaking. Charcot found that in hypnosis the man had perfectly normal control of his limbs. It proved that the nervous system had not been destroyed by the lightening strike, and that the problem must be in the mind. It also shows that giving a condition a name, does not enhance one's understanding of it.

As a young lecturer at the University of Vienna, Freud obtained a bursary on which he went to study under Charcot in Paris. He told Charcot about Breuer's discovery of catharsis. Charcot showed no interest in that discovery. It is not surprising that Freud did not pursue the matter, because Freud had gone to study under Charcot, not to teach him anything. Charcot, however thought highly of Freud, and asked him to write a paper on the differences between somatic and psychic paralyses. That paper was ultimately written by Freud in French. It has long since been available in English, but was only translated into German near the end of the last century.

The two main points made in that paper are, that a psychically paralysed leg is dragged, rather than swung, and that if as much as one toe can be moved on a paralysed leg, the paralysis is psychic, rather than somatic.

PREAMBLE

Before we can really start, we need to have a close look at the difference between the two words "effect" and "affect". They seem almost like identical twins. They are both about the consequence of an event, but they are very different.

Brought up on science, the latter day public is well versed in the concept of cause and effect. Everybody knows what an effect is. It is one of the consequences of a cause, but effect may not be the only consequence of that one cause. The cause may also produce an affect.

If you are rock solid on the difference between effect and affect, read no further. Go straight to Chapter 1, but you need to be very sure about the difference, because this book is about the two routes which the affect can take in an individual. Which route the affect takes, depends on how it is handled. To those, who decide to persevere with this chapter, I will explain the difference between effect and affect, even to the point of labouring it.

If you hit an iron nail with a hammer, the effect is merely that the nail penetrates further into the wood. There is no affect. Neither the wood nor the iron, nail have any feelings. All the consequences of the blow are logical.

If, on the other hand (please pardon the pun) you hit a fingernail with a hammer, there is both effect and affect. The effect is that you feel pain, the tissue under the fingernail is contused, blood seeps out of the little blood vessels, and the fingernail turns black.

All that is bad enough, but the affect goes much further. The affect is that you are shocked, you get angry with yourself, you feel incompetent, throw the hammer across the room, smash the mirror on the wall, and decide to give up carpentry.

The blow on the fingernail has had an effect on your finger, and has affected you as a person. The consequences of the former are very logical, but the consequences of the latter are very human and illogical. Then the impact of the hammer on the mirror only has a logical effect. The glass breaks, but the sight and sound of what you have done, has yet another affect on you. What that affect is, depends on you.

Affect is how you feel about what has happened, or at least how you should feel about what has happened. Unfortunately the feeling about what has happened may be smothered, or may never even get the chance to arise. This book is about the consequences of those suppressed or repressed feelings. Those consequences can be far reaching. They amount to emotional constipation. That emotional constipation may change your life and it may last a life time, unless it is discharged. The discharge is called catharsis.

Chapter 1 - REASONABLENESS

G.K.Chesterton, who was a famous writer in his day, once said: *"The real trouble with this world of ours is not that it is an unreasonable one. The trouble is that it is nearly reasonable, but not quite."*

Since the world itself simply obeys the inexorable laws of the universe, what part of it is not quite reasonable? The answer to that question is very simple. The part of the world that is not quite reasonable is the human race. In fact most people are unreasonable some of the time, and some people are unreasonable most of the time.

That it is not news, and it is well summed up in the typically Yorkshire saying: *"All the world's queer save thee and me, and even thou art a bit peculiar".* On the assumption that my present reader will temporarily stand in for the typical Yorkshireman, it is true to say that we are all a bit peculiar, and some are more peculiar than others.

Regrettably neither Chesterton, nor the archetypal Yorkshireman, have told us why some people are peculiar or unreasonable. They have not told us why some people are driven, why some are obsessive, and why others suffer strange illnesses from "unknown viruses". Believe it or not, I shall answer all those questions for you.

To enable you to understand what I have to say, we shall need a common vocabulary. The dictionary for that common vocabulary is at the back of this book. The first word to be looked up there is "Resistance

If you happen to have a psycho-neurosis, resistance has already been in operation. Your subconscious mind is much quicker than you are. As soon as it realised, that if you go further into this subject, you will be in serious danger of recalling one of your own traumatic memories, resistance will have gone into overdrive.

Your subconscious mind knows, that if you read on you might inadvertently recall a repressed experience. Then you might stumble into the very emotion which you have been struggling to avoid for years. Your subconscious mind will try to protect you from that unwelcome eventuality

Unfortunately, flight from the emotion associated with a traumatic experience, gives you emotional constipation. The consequence of emotional constipation is the queerness, which Yorkshire folk see in each other, and that is the reason why the world is *"nearly reasonable, but not quite"*.

I have to hope that you are bold enough to read on. You should read on, because with the passage of time, any previously terrifying or embarrassing experience, will turn out to be a paper tiger.

Chapter 2 - THE SUBCONSCIOUS MIND

The explanation for the unreasonableness spotted by G.K.Chesterton, and the queerness noticed by Yorkshire folk among each other, has its roots in the <u>subconscious mind.</u>

You are well aware that you have a <u>conscious mind</u>. You are thinking with it as you read these lines, but the field of view of your conscious mind is very limited. Your conscious mind knows what you are seeing, hearing, smelling, touching, tasting or thinking just now. All told, that is not a lot.

Compared to your conscious mind, your subconscious mind is vast. You do not spend a lot of time thinking with your conscious mind about your subconscious, but the subconscious is thinking about you all the time. It stores a tremendous amount of information, and it guards you when you are asleep, as well as when you are awake.

Your conscious mind tends to give you the impression that it is all there is to you, and that it has everything under control. Quite the opposite is the case. It is the subconscious, which is the real you, and it does most of your work for you. Usually it does that with lightening speed.

When your subconscious falters in its task, you get a glimpse into the mechanics of your mind. If you want to remember something, which you should know very well, but you can not recall it at that moment, the relationship between the conscious mind and the subconscious has temporarily broken down. At that point you cannot tell, whether you will ever be able to recall the missing fact, name or telephone number. Yet five minutes or an hour later, the missing fact suddenly pops unbidden into your conscious mind.

That is the work of the subconscious. While you were busy, working with your conscious mind in going about your daily tasks, the subconscious has done five jobs for you. It has remembered that you wanted a certain name. It has searched for that name. It finally found that name. Then it selected an opportune moment, and lastly it presented the missing name to the conscious mind.

The essential thing to realise is that your subconscious is working away all the time. Its existence is not as obvious as the existence of your conscious mind, but it is constantly at work. It works away when you are awake, and while you are asleep. It works away, whether you want it to or not. It guards you constantly, and it also has regard to your wishes. There are some things which you want to remember, and there are some things, which you would rather not remember. The subconscious takes your preferences on board, even if your conscious mind is not really aware of your preferences. That is often a very useful service, but sometimes the subconscious overdoes it. When that happens, you get a psycho-neurosis, more easily understood as "emotional constipation".

Chapter 3 - A PARADOX

A paradox, says the Oxford English Dictionary: "is some fact which is contrary to received opinion or belief". That word also implies a correct opinion, even if that opinion is contrary to common sense. Amnesia is such a paradox.

Amnesia is the name given to the state of affairs, when someone ought to know something, but has absolutely no recollection of it. Such amnesia often sets in after a car crash. The driver may remember very clearly what happened just before the crash, and very precisely what happened just after the crash, but despite the tangible evidence of the wreckage, he has absolutely no recollection of the crash itself. Recollection of that incident is blocked.

Most people's immediate reaction to such amnesia is: "Pull the other one. It's got bells on it." People tend to think, that the driver is only claiming that he can't remember, because he does not want to admit his guilt. That is a natural reaction to such amnesia, because the loss of memory of such an important event is a paradox. Common sense says that the incident ought to have imprinted itself on the memory, but the driver says that he does not remember anything about it. That is the paradox. It is paradoxical that there may be memories stored in your own mind, which you can not recall. It is even harder to accept that there may be important events stored in the deepest recesses of another person's mind, which he or she can not recall.

You may very well claim that you have no such irretrievable memories. It would be tempting to challenge you by saying: "Remember something that you can't remember", but that would be absurd. You could not find the thing you can't remember, because you can't remember it. You can't think of it, because for some strange reason, in some mysterious way, access to that memory is blocked.

Nevertheless, it is almost inevitable that you have had some unwelcome experiences, which you chose to "put out of your mind". Those memories have not ceased to exist. They are there in your data banks, and the more they bothered you at the time, the more they are recorded, but you may not be able to recall them. You may not even know that they are there. They are concealed by amnesia.

That is the great paradox. You may know something in the sense that you know it to be true if you are reminded of it, but do not know it in the sense that you could not voluntarily recall it. Such a "forgotten" memory may be recollected, if it happens to be brought to your attention by some set of external circumstances, like an undeniable photograph.

The words know, remember, recall and recollect are often used interchangeably, but they do have different shades of meaning. You "know" something if the data is electronically stored in your data cells. You can be said to "remember" something, if a fact like your own name, which you "know" is also constantly available to your conscious mind. You "recall" something, if you can drag the data out of your subconscious at will by your own efforts. You recollect something, if external circumstances force you to retrieve a memory of which you would not otherwise be aware. When that happens you might say: "Now that you mention it..... "

The different ways in which a memory can come back into your conscious mind are not paradoxical. We experience them all the time. The paradox is that there can be a record of an incident in your data banks, but you have absolutely no recollection of it. Such amnesia may be partial, in the sense that the memory suddenly surfaces at odd moments, and disappears equally suddenly. Alternatively the amnesia may be total.

The purpose of this book is to make you aware of three facts. The astonishing news is that, under the stress of strong emotions, an unwelcome memory may be so effectively suppressed by an effort of will power, that it remains suppressed. It is then said to be repressed.

The bad news is that if a memory is so effectively repressed as to drive its nerve signals completely out of the mind into the body, then that innervation will be converted into bodily symptoms. In that way a repressed memory may cause psycho-somatic symptoms (i.e. an illness). If the repression is not quite complete, the rogue innervation from the repressed memory may cause psychic disturbances like obsession, phobia or paranoia. Finally, but by no means least, the repressed memory may cause behavioural problems, may effect decision taking or produce attitudes, which can seriously affect your life

The good news is that such a repressed memory, which you are quite unable to recall in the normal waking state (however hard you try), may come back to you in the course of a hypnoid state, and will almost certainly come back to you in hypnosis. When that happens, you will become fully aware of the paradox. You "knew" a fact, but you did not know that you "knew" it.

If you recollect such a repressed memory, and discharge the emotion attached to it, the psycho-somatic illness, psychic disturbance or behavioural disorder, which it produced, disappears instantly. The affliction disappears, because the rogue innervation, which produced it, and maintained it, no longer exists. It has been discharged by the release of the emotion, which originally made the thought so unwelcome that it was intolerable, and caused you to repress it.

The memory of the relevant event remains. It is then retrievable at will. That widens your store of useable experience, but the rogue innervation springing from the constant repression has been purged from the mind. When that rogue innervation is gone, so is the affect (see chapter 5) which it had on you. That purging of the rogue innervation from the mind is called CATHARSIS.

Chapter 4 - CATHARSIS

Catharsis is really nothing new. As a vague realisation it has always been accepted. It was practised by the Israelites when they ritually sent a goat into the desert to carry away their sins. People who participated in the ritual could "get guilt off their chest". The scapegoat will undoubtedly have carried some people's guilt away into the desert, but that guilt had not been on their chest. It had been in the subconscious parts of their mind.

Catharsis is practised by the Chinese, when they smash plates at the Chinese New Year celebrations. Catharsis is practised by the Greeks, when they smash crockery at weddings. Somewhat more indirectly, catharsis was practised by the Jews, when they hired women to wail at funerals. The wailing of the women created an atmosphere in which the genuine mourners were able to "let go", and discharge their grief with real tears. Under cover of the cacophony made by the paid wailers the bereaved were able to achieve catharsis.

In the clinical sense, catharsis was discovered in Vienna towards the end of the Victorian era by Dr.Josef Breuer, and confirmed by the neurologist Dr Sigmund Freud. The discovery was at first published in a scientific paper called "Preliminary Communications" and later in a book called "Studies on Hysteria" to which Breuer and Freud contributed separate cases histories and comments.

At that time, it was already well recognised that certain physical illnesses had their origins in the nervous system. In consequence, such illnesses were assigned to neurologists, who called them hysteria. That is not to be confused with hysterics, a display of emotions, to which young Victorian ladies were particularly prone. Such hysterics were sometimes called "the vapours". Hysteria, on the other hand, was quite the opposite, because it involved a suppression of emotion.

Hysterics, by whatever name, have largely disappeared from the social scene, but Hysteria is still with us on all sides today. Nowadays it is called psycho-somatic illness. That term is composed of the Greek words for "mind" and "body" to indicate an affliction of the body, which has no other origin than electronic signals sent to the body from the mind. Since the symptoms are solely caused by messages from the mind, when those signals stop, the symptoms stop too. Dr.Josef Breuer discovered that startling fact in the course of his treatment of a young lady called Bertha Pappenheim. She achieved lasting fame in the Studies on Hysteria under the alias "Anna O".

Dr.Breuer's discovery was a lucky accident, like the discovery of penicillin by Dr.Alexander Fleming. In both those cases the accidental discovery was made by minds large enough to realise the significance of what they saw. Dr.Fleming happened to notice that bacteria would not multiply in areas of his cultures at places where the cultures were contaminated by fungus. Fleming was able to repeat that experiment, and thus confirm his finding.

Dr.Breuer was even more lucky with the circumstances of his discovery. One can not normally repeat catharsis in a patient. Once the traumatic memory has been recalled, and the relevant emotion has been discharged, the symptoms are gone. They can not be restored, but Bertha Pappenheim had the talent (or misfortune) of being able to give herself new symptoms, by repressing new guilty fantasies as soon as the previous symptoms had been cleared up by catharsis. It enabled Breuer to repeat the "Talking Cure" with that patient, and thus confirm his findings.

Josef Breuer told his young friend Sigmund Freud about his discovery. Freud tried Breuer's method of curing psycho-somatic symptoms for himself, and persuaded Breuer to agree to publication of their findings. The preliminary communications which they issued, disclosed the discovery in a sentence of truly Germanic length. They wrote: *"We found to our great surprise at first, that each individual hysterical (psycho-somatic) symptom immediately and permanently disappeared when we had succeeded in bringing clearly to light the memory of the event by which it was provoked and in arousing its accompanying affect, and when the patient had described that event in the greatest possible detail and had put that affect into words."* They added, that if the relevant affect is not discharged or the event described, recall by itself (usually) has no effect.

At that stage their findings were confined to cases of psycho-somatic illness, that is to say, to cases in which the innervation from the repressed trauma has been driven out of the psyche into the soma. Freud later found that the same mechanism of symptom production and cure operated in cases of obsession, phobia and paranoia. In such cases the innervation from the repressed thought is not driven out of the mind into the body. It stays in the mind, and disturbs normal, rational behaviour.

In the century since that epoch making discovery, it has been found by thousands of hypno and psycho-therapists, that the same mechanism of repression operates in the production of behavioural disorders of every conceivable kind. In cases of behavioural disorders the incident is sometimes recalled, but the relevant emotion has not been discharged. Once the incident is fully recalled, and the previously unbearable emotion is discharged by overt physical action like tears, overt anger, speech or even laughter, the behavioural disorders disappear permanently.

✳✳✳✳✳✳✳✳

"There are more things in heaven and earth than are dreamt of in your philosophy."...............

Shakespeare – Hamlet 1.5

FLOW DIAGRAM

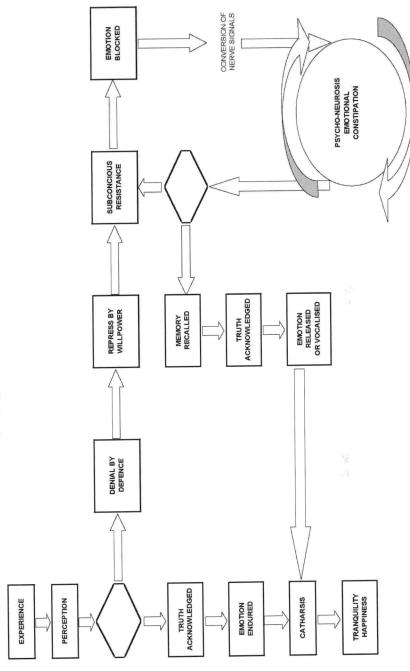

Diag. 1 - FLOWCHART

Emotional constipation, which is colloquially spoken of as a block or a hang-up, is in effect a loop. It manifests itself by repeated interference; either with normal body function or with specific every- day thought processes. That is called psycho-neurosis.

Chapter 5 - AFFECT (Psycho-somatic symptoms)

In the diagram overleaf I have attempted to set out the sequence of steps involved in the repression of a memory, and the conversion of its nerve impulses into a psycho-somatic illness, as discovered by Josef Breuer in the course of his treatment of Bertha Pappenheim.. The rogue innervation in the brain, caused by the repression of the unendurable thought, produces the physical symptoms of a psycho-neurosis in the body.

Such psycho-somatic symptoms are not imaginary. They are very real. The skin may become oversensitive, worn joints may become inflamed, or a limb may become completely paralysed The paralysis caused by signals from the brain, telling the limb not to move, is a different matter to the paralysis caused by cutting the nerve fibres from the brain to the limb. In this latter case the cut prevents any order from the brain to the limb, from ever getting through to the limb. In the former case the order to keep the limb paralysed does keep getting through to the limb, but a psycho-somatic paralysis is just as real as an organic one.

There are three forms of such psycho-somatic symptoms. The rogue nerve impulses stemming from the repressed trauma may simply seize on an existing symptom from an ongoing infection, from a recent injury or from a genetic weakness, and emphasise it. In that way the rogue nerve signals can exaggerate a minor ache from normal wear and tear into excruciating pain.

Alternatively, the rogue innervation may produce symptoms of its own, which resemble the symptoms of some known physical disease. That may lead to misdiagnosis of the psycho-somatic affect as an organic illness. In such a case the mistake can be spotted by the fact that the prescribed medication, which normally takes swift effect, has no effect whatever.

Thirdly, the rogue innervation may produce an unrecognisable syndrome of symptoms, which is then often ascribed to an "unknown virus". In such a case the doctor is probably right. It probably is a virus, but it is an electronic virus, similar to a computer virus.

It is much easier to write this chapter today than it would have been twenty years ago, because the public is now generally computer literate. They know what a computer virus is. Things were very different in 1895, when Josef Breuer wrote his contribution to the Studies on Hysteria. In those days electric lights in the home were a novelty, and electricity was a mystery. At that time Breuer had to write: *"I shall scarcely be suspected of identifying nervous excitation with electricity, if I return once more to comparison with an electrical system".* Today we know that nervous excitation can indeed be identified with electricity. We now know that it can be measure in tens of millivolts. Those millivolts propel electric currents to and from the brain, and such electric currents flow in the brain as they do in the hardware of a computer. It is that flow of currents which constitute the mind.

Nowadays we can not escape the thought that there is an analogy between the brain and a computer. Both hold data electronically. Both do calculations with that data, both retrieve data by scanning through the data banks, and both display the product of their work on a screen. In the case of human beings, that screen is what we recognise as conscious thought. On that basis we can regard the anatomical substance of the brain as the computer hardware. The mind on the other hand has no anatomy. It consists solely of the electronic functioning of the brain. It is the software to which we add as we go along. That makes us the people we are. That gives us our personality. It may be possible to clone human beings. In that case the young clone will have the same hardware as the parent clone, but he or she will be a very different personality. The young clone will have different experiences, and will consequently build up different software. (*)

The thing about software is that you can introduce a computer virus into it. In a computer that is done by writing and loading a short program into the software. That extra program instructs the computer to do some specific thing, designed to interfere with the normal working of the computer. In the mind the virus is introduced by an exertion of will power, telling the mind not to recall a certain fact, because it does not want it to be true. That creates a denial or a daydream. It thereby transfers the experience into the safety of a hypnoid state, but the mind knows that it knows that fact, and can not shut it off. All it can do is to send the nerve signals elsewhere, but it has not been given any instructions on where to send them. Somewhere they will find the path of least resistance. In extreme cases that nerve signal escapes from the brain into the body, and does some mischief there. It may cause an itch or pain or throw the endocrine system off kilter. In short it can produce the symptoms of a physical illness.

(*) Identical twins are clones. The similarity of their personalities is not only due to the fact that they have the same genes, but also due to the fact that they usually grow up in almost identical environments. That would change, if they were sitting in the back of a car, one looking out to the left and the other to the right. If one of them fleetingly saw a horrific accident in which a child was crushed by a bus and disembowelled, that twin might say to itself: "I do not believe what I have seen. It can not be true. I did not really see that at all" That twin might then go into denial, thereby giving itself one of the infinite number of possible affects. It would then be a very different person from its twin

✷✷✷✷✷✷✷✷

Sleeping Beauty pricked her finger on a thorn (Trauma), and was spellbound.
German Fable

✷✷✷✷✷✷✷✷

LIST OF SOME PSYCHO-SOMATIC AFFLICTIONS

Some of the syndromes listed below may be of organic origin. As such their manifestations may be exaggerated by a parallel psycho-somatic affect.

The list of the syndromes set out below does not purport to be exhaustive. There is no way in which it could be made exhaustive, because the admixture of symptoms, which the mind could produce as an "Unknown Virus", is infinite

ALLERGY
ALOPECIA
ANGER
ANOREXIA
ANORGASMIA
ARTHRITIS
ASTHMA
BEDWETTING
BLUSHING
BRUXISM
BULIMIA
CHAS. BONNET SYNDROME
CHEWING LIPS
CHRONIC PAIN
COLITIS
CRAMP
CYSTITIS
DEPRESSION
EMETOPHOBIA
FAILURE TO HEAL
FRIGIDITY
GLOBUS HYSTERICUS
HEADACHES
HYPERTENSION
IMMUNE SYSTEM DISORDER
IMPOTENCE
INCONTINENCE
INFERTILITY

IRRITABLE BOWEL SYNDROME
INSOMNIA
LOSS OF SPEECH
LUPUS ERYTHEMATOSUS
MIGRAINE
NAUSEA
NEURITIS
PALPITATIONS
PARALYSIS
PARASOMNIA
PSORIASIS
RESTLESS LEG SYNDROME
SHY BLADDER
SKIN PICKING DISORDER
SKIN CONDITIONS
SLEEP DISORDERS
SOMNAMBULISM
SQUINT
STUTTERING
SWEATING
TICS/TWITCHES
TINNITUS
TUSSI NERVOSA
VAGINISMUS
VOMITING
WALLEYE

Chapter 6 - AFFECT (Psychic Disturbance)

We now come to cases where the exertion of will power was not so forceful that the resultant innervation caused physical illness. The nerve signals stay in the mind where they cause psychic disorders like phobias, obsessions or paranoia, by behaving like a computer virus.

The virus we discussed in the previous chapter is not a chemical substance. It is an electronic pattern of instructions, like a computer virus. That is to say, it consists solely of electronic signals passing through the hardware of the brain. There is no essential difference between it and the other electronic signals, which together constitute our minds. The only difference is that will power caused the mind to accept software instructions to act as if a certain fact did not exist.

Such instructions, given by force of stress, causing a hypnoid state for fear (*) of an emotional upheaval, may seem perverse. They fly in the face of reality, and create nonsensical results, but they may have been necessary to protect the body from an overload of adrenaline. The consequent psychic disturbance does not mean that the individuals afflicted by such psychic disturbances are mentally defective. On the contrary, they are people with great will power, whose brain is in perfect working order. It is just obeying the instruction which it was given in a moment of extreme stress, to protect the body from an emotional overload

Like the hardware of a computer, the brain simply carries out electronically the electronic instructions which it has received. The trouble is that the brain did not receive <u>enough</u> instructions. A man who has a psychic disorder, which compels him to wash his hands one hundred and fifty times per day, is not mentally defective. His problem is merely that, in the panic which caused the repression, he has given himself a computer virus, without telling his brain what to do with the nerve signals arising from the repressed incident.

Such a loose nerve signal has to go somewhere. It is then channelled into some activity or affect, chosen at random by the nerve impulses themselves. They will probably go down the path of least resistance. Once an escape route for the rogue nerve signals has been found, those signals are likely to keep going down the same path, repeatedly causing the same affect - hand washing - hand washing - hand washing.

The list of possible obsessions is endless. The same is true of phobias. Their aetiology is the same as that of obsessions, and the list of phobias is infinite. Some of them are listed below. Such phobias, paranoia and obsessions, however queer they may seem to our archetypal Yorkshireman, do not show that you are crazy. What they do show very clearly, is that you have a repressed memory or emotion, acting as a computer virus in a perfect brain.

(*) Fear gives rise to the three Fs – Fight, Flight or Freeze. This book is about Freeze.

ARBITRARY LIST OF SOME POSSIBLE PHOBIAS

An animal	Zoophobia
Animal skin	Doraphobia
Bacteria	Bacteriophobia or Microbiophobia
Beards	Pogonophobia
Bees	Apiphobia ormelissophobia
Being alone	Autophobia
Birds	Ornithophobia
Blood	Haematophobia
Blushing	Erithophobia
Books	Bibliophobia
Cats	Allurophobia or gatophobia
Chickens	Alectorophobia
Children	Pediophobia
China	Sinophobia
Churches	Ecclesiaphobia
Colours	Chromatophobia
Corpse	Necrophobia
Crossing a bridge	Gephyrophobia
Crowds	Ochlophobia
Dampness	Hygrophobia
Darkness	Achluophobia or nyctophobia
Death	Necrophobia
Deformity	Dysmorphophobia
Dogs	Cynophobia
Dolls	Pediophobia
Drinking	Dipsophobia
Drugs	Pharmacophobia
Electricity	Electrophobia
Elevated places	Acrophobia
Empty rooms	Kenophobia
Enclosed spaces	Claustrophobia
Everything	Panophobia
Faeces	Coprophobia
Feathers	Pteronophobia
Fire	Pyrophobia
Flowers	Anthophobia
Foreigners	Xenophobia
Glass	Crystallphobia
Horses	Hippophobia
Humans	Anthropophobia
Insects	Entomophobia

Knees	Genuphobia
Light	Photophobia
Machinery	Mechanophobia
Men	Androphobia
Microbes	Bacilliphobia
Mirrors	Eisoptrophobia
Nakedness	Gymnophobia
Oneself	Autophobia
Open spaces	Agoraphobia or Kenophobia
Pleasure	Hedonophobia
Poverty	Peniaphobia
Pregnancy	Maieusiophobia
Precipices	Cremnophobia
Rain	Ombrophobia
Reptiles	Batrachophobia
Rivers	Potamophobia
Sacred things	Hierophobia
Sex	Genophobia
Sexual intercourse	Coitophobia
Skin	Dermatophobia
Sleep	Hypnophobia
Smell	Olfactophobia
Snakes	Ophidiophobia
Society	Anthropophobia
Sound	Akousticophobia
Sourness	Acerophobia
Speaking aloud	Phonphobia
Speed	Tachophobia
Spiders	Arachnophobia
Spirits	Demonophobia
Stealing	Cleptophobia
Strangers	Xenophobia
Sun	Heliophobia
Swallowing	Phagephobia
Teeth	Odontophobia
Thirteen at table	Triskaidekaphobia
Trees	Dendrophobia
Uncovered body	Gymnophobia
Vomiting	Emetophobia
Wind	Anemophobia
Women	Gynophobia
Worms	Helminthophobia
Wounds	Traumatophobia

Chapter 7 - Affect (Behaviour Disorder)

This chapter is the most difficult, because the variety of behavioural disorders is infinite. What they all have in common is that the sufferer is driven. He is either driven to keep doing something which common sense tells him not to do, or he is driven to shy away from doing something which common sense tells him he should be doing. In either case it is the innervation from a repressed emotion, which provides the driving force. What makes the various behavioural disorders seem so different from each other, is that the affect, selected at random by the sufferer's subconscious as the outlet for that innervation, is so very different in each case. The sufferers are all "queer" in very different ways, but they are all queer for the same reason. We are now deep into the territory of the archetypal Yorkshireman.

Depression, self-mutilation and externalisation are three categories of such queer behaviour. There are only two points that can usefully be made on the subject of depression. Few things are as depressing as the continuous subconscious exertion of keeping a memory in repression. The other is that the successful recollection of the relevant repressed memory makes the depression dissolve just like morning mist in summer sunshine - only more quickly.

Self-mutilation and externalisation, on the other hand, could take up many pages of many books, but they are simply the reverse and obverse of the same problem. In self-mutilation the sufferers seek to use up the loose rogue innervation on themselves. In externalisation the sufferers expend the innervation on the outside world. Either way they are driven.

There is no limit to the variety of methods of self-mutilation. It includes any activity, which is harmful to the wellbeing of the body of the psycho-neurotic. It ranges from biting the fingernail to putting a silver stud through the tongue, from getting tattooed to slashing the arms with razor blades, from excessive smoking, which leads to lung cancer, to excessive eating, whish leads to obesity and heart failure. All those activities harm the body. In respect of all of them you could ask the sufferer: ***"Why do you keep doing it, when you know that..........? - Why ?"***

Sufferers can never answer that rational question, because the answer is irrational. The answer is irrational, because it is not the <u>effect</u> of the incident that gave rise to the irrational behaviour, but the very personal <u>affect</u> to which the incident had on the individual. Hence the answer is that they are driven by the loose innervation from their repressed traumatic memory, which finds an outlet in that self-mutilating activity. Bothered by the nervous excitation, the smoker subconsciously says to himself: "If I just have another cigarette, I will feel better". The fat woman, who is always talking about dieting, subconsciously says to herself: "If I just have another biscuit, I shall feel better". It's not true. They are all just as mistaken as the dried-out junky who "decides" to have another shot of heroin. It will not make him feel better.

What he and the fat woman, and the chain-smoker need to do, is to recollect their respective traumatic memories, and discharge the relevant emotions. They have to let their feelings go.

The same self-deception, discussed above, operates in cases of externalisation. In such cases also, the sufferer is driven. There, the sufferer uses up the loose innervation on his environment instead of on himself. He may smash a plate glass window, or pull up the hyacinths in the Corporation's parks instead of mutilating himself. The externalisation may even have the appearance of being socially beneficial, if it is coupled with identification.

Identification occurs when the externaliser picks on someone or some animal to "help", instead of smashing a window. "If I just keep collecting money for charity, and reach my target, I shall feel better". What an externaliser is driven to do in his environment may seem harmful or may seem beneficial. He may bully his school mates, or he may "make a thing" of helping old ladies across busy roads. In either case he subconsciously says to himself: "If I just do that, I shall feel better".

To comment on such behaviour as "good" or "bad" would be judgmental. It is neither good nor bad. In psycho-therapeutic terms such actions can not be judged, because they are irrational. They are not determined by reason, but by loose nerve impulses. Whether they seem "good" or "bad" makes a difference to how the world reacts to the sufferer, but in both cases they are bad for the sufferer, because they are his prison.

Externalisation can also be the cause of extremism, and of most other -isms. The sufferer is driven to solve one or other of the world's insoluble problems. The more insoluble the problems are the better, because in that way the externaliser will not run out of his adopted cause. If the cause does run out, the externaliser will instantly find another one. The rogue innervation must be kept busy. The externaliser is always subconsciously saying to himself: "If I just solve that problem (for somebody else, of course) I shall feel better.

What he means is, that if he keeps busy with his cause, the repressed memory can not surface. Some externalisers give their life to, or for, their adopted cause. To all of them one is inclined to say: "Get a life", but one would have to do more than that. It is no more use telling them to "get a life" than it is to tell someone with a psychic paralysis in a leg to walk normally. One would have to tell them <u>how</u> to do it. One would have to tell them to take steps to retrieve the traumatic memory, which they have been repressing for long enough. One would have to tell them, but they would not listen. Resistance sees to that (see Chapter 11)

Chapter 8 - INDIRECT AFFECT AND TOTALITY OF STRESS

Some years ago the U.S.Navy conducted a survey on sick sailors. They discovered that healthy young sailors fell ill, when they had received stressful news from home. If a loved parent died, if his baby was ill, or if his wife had run away with another man, the sailor was liable to fall ill with some recognisable infection. It had to be concluded that stress had damaged his immune system.

From day to day, our immune system takes care of our bodies, and mops up intruders. The world is full of bacteria and viruses, which constantly try to intrude into our bodies. That happens all the time, and the immune system deals with them all the time, unless something intervenes and undermines the immune system. The U.S. Navy's survey confirmed, what can be inferred from everyday observation, that stress can damage the immune system.

If the stress stems from external circumstances, it will sooner or later resolve itself. If the stress is from a repressed memory, it will last as long as the repression lasts, and that may last for a life time. Another fact which must be taken into account, is that stresses are cumulative. If the subconscious mind is not encumbered with the stress of a repressed memory, then stress from a current disaster may just get shrugged off, but if there is ongoing stress from a long repressed memory, the extra stress from daily life may just be enough to damage the immune system. In those circumstances the person is vulnerable to bacterial attack. He or she may then fall ill like any other patient, but only because the totality of stress overwhelmed the immune system.

Totality of stress serves to explain another puzzling phenomenon. It is usually children and young people who succumb to psycho-somatic afflictions from incidents, which seem traumatic to them (not necessarily to anyone else). Young children are particularly vulnerable to such affects, because at their tender age their emotions are sometimes too fierce for them to handle. Nevertheless, people who suffer a serious trauma in their childhood usually seem to "get over it", and lead healthy and successful lives.

If , on the other hand, they did repress the memory of their traumatic experience, the relevant innervation will inevitably have had some effect on their thought processes, (see Chapter 19) That effect on their thought processes need not have produced any visible harmful affect at that stage. It may indeed have had a beneficial effect. They may have been driven in their work, and thereby become successful. Later, when some disaster like bankruptcy or divorce befalls them, they may fall ill. Alternatively, they may develop a psychic or behavioural disorder, like depression, for which there is no other rational explanation.

In such cases, no amount if tinkering with the later trauma will resolve the problem. When the childhood trauma is recollected, and abreacted in hypnosis, the affect from the childhood trauma, which only became manifest at the time of the bankruptcy, disappears. Then, the problems from the bankruptcy are still as stressful as before, but the totality of stress has been reduced by the removal of the stress from the childhood trauma.

A similar effect, (or rather affect) can be seen in people who get disproportionately (i.e. hysterically) distressed by one of life's little dramas. The extra temporary stress from the little drama, added to the constant stress from their long repressed trauma, drives then temporarily over the edge of normal behaviour. In that way totality of stress explains many phenomena, which are inexplicable on the basis of a single causative factor.

****

There is an understandable temptation to think that people who succumb to psycho-neurosis must be weak characters of low intellect. The opposite is the case. "Among hysterics (i.e. victims of psycho-neurosis) may be found people of the clearest intellect, strongest will, greatest character and highest critical powers"
Preliminary Communication by Breuer and Freud 1893

****

Chapter 9 - TYPES OF NEUROSES (Psychic, Somatic and Threshold of Affect)

By the last decade of Queen Victoria's reign, doctors were well aware of bacteria, parasites and viruses as the causes of illness. They were also aware, that certain illnesses had no such cause. Because those illnesses seemed to be connected with the nervous system, they became the province of neurologists, and were called neuroses.

Although neurologists did designate some manifestations of neuroses as "Hysteria" (not to be confused with hysterics) they were largely working in the dark. When Josef Breuer discovered that the repression of a traumatic thought could cause bodily illness (Hysteria), a bright light suddenly shone into the murky subject of neuroses. Concurrently, Breuer also discovered that the hysteria disappeared as suddenly, and as mysteriously, as it had appeared, if the repressed memory was recollected, and described in detail. The realisation that hysterias could be cleared up by the "Talking Cure", nowadays called hypno-analysis, transformed the scene at a stroke.

Since the problem had evidently been in the mind, such neuroses came to be called psycho-neuroses. Other afflictions of the nervous system, which were clearly neuroses, did not respond to Breuer's form of psycho-therapy. Their source and effect seemed to be entirely in the body. They were called neuresthenia. Working as a neurologist (not as a psychologist) Freud divided neuresthenia into two groups. He called one group Anxiety Neurosis, and the other group Neuresthenia proper. The latter is nowadays called Chronic Fatigue Syndrome or Myalgic Encephalomyelitis, or just ME. The former group he attributed to inadequate sexual satisfaction, and the latter to masturbation.

Whether or not the aetiology of those somatic neuroses was correctly understood, the list of their potential effects and affects is formidable, and in cases of that type of anxiety neurosis, potentially life threatening. This book, however, is about psycho-neuroses. I neither need to, nor do I want to, go into the aetiology of somatic neuroses. Just two points need to be made, which relate to psycho-neuroses, as much as they do to somatic neuroses. They are really more than points. They are concepts.

The first of those two concepts is the threshold concept. That is not a matter of "cause and effect", but of "cause and affect". We all have different constitutions. Some people can jump five feet high, others can barely jump five inches. Some people can be immersed in cold water for five hours. At the same temperature, others would die of hypothermia within five minutes. Such differences can also be found in the ability of people to withstand nervous stress. Some people can take a lot of nervous stress. Others can only take very little. The fact that many people get no ill effect from masturbation, does not mean that nobody gets any ill effect from that activity. Similarly, some people may be able to repress a psychic trauma without any visible ill affect, whereas others seem to succumb at once to the stress from a similar psychic trauma.

The second concept is the notion of mixed neuroses. On the supposition that neuroses are either psychic or somatic, it should not be possible to resolve or relieve the symptoms of a somatic neurosis by means of hypno-analysis. On that supposition, a hypno-therapist would have to decide on the cause of the symptoms, before attempting an analysis. That approach is not necessarily correct, because a somatic neurosis and a psycho-neurosis may be running side by side. In such a case, removal of the psycho-neurosis would not only be beneficial in itself. It would also reduce the totality of stress (see Chapter 8). Another possibility is that the psycho-neurosis may have adopted the symptoms of the somatic neurosis, and exaggerated them. In that case removal of the psycho-neurosis would reduce the symptoms of the somatic neurosis to normal levels.

The third possibility is that the psycho-neurosis adopted the symptoms of the somatic neurosis, but that the somatic neurosis was subsequently resolved. The symptoms which are left may have all the hallmarks of the original somatic neurosis, but may in fact be a psycho-neurosis. Those symptoms are meanwhile sustained by the psycho-neurosis, and can therefore be resolved by hypno-analysis.

The importance of the totality of stress, discussed in the previous chapter, is that an individual's threshold of tolerance will only be crossed, when the totality of stress is too great for him to endure. Until then there will be no evident affect. A girl may have a traumatic experience at the age of five. (See Chapter 13) but there may be no outward manifestation of the trauma, because the threshold of tolerance has not been crossed. Then, following another trauma later in life, there may be persistent headaches, because the totality of stress from continued repression of the old childhood trauma, plus the stress from the current problem, happen to exceed the tolerance threshold of that individual.

Similarly a boy of six may have a traumatic experience which he apparently shrugs off. ("children are so resilient" !!!) He may grow up and run a successful business. The success may indeed be due to the fact that he is driven by the psycho-neurosis from his trauma, but there is no outward sign of any ill affect. When the business runs into trouble, instead of dealing with the problem effectively, the man may go into a serious depression. In that case the current stress of the business, plus the ongoing stress of the old trauma, have created a totality of stress which exceeds that individual's own particular threshold of stress tolerance.

In that way, old unresolved affects of childhood traumas have three effects. They reduce the efficiency of the day to day functioning of the mind, they will undoubtedly add to the level of stress experienced in daily life, and they increase the likelihood of psycho-somatic affects manifesting themselves, when the stresses of everyday life, plus the stress of the repressed childhood trauma exceed that particular individual's threshold of stress tolerance.

Chapter 10 - ASSOCIATION OF IDEAS

Not long ago, chemists still explained molecular structure with the aid of simple models. They used solid wooden balls to represent atoms, and little wooden sticks to join them into molecules. In reality atoms are not solid spheres, and when they combine into molecules they clump tightly together so tightly, that they distort each other's shape. Although the wooden models were a crude imitation of reality, they made it easy to explain molecular structure, like those of graphite and diamond. In graphite each carbon atom is only joined to three other carbon atoms. In that way carbon can form sheets of pure carbon molecules. Those sheets can easily be rubbed off each other. That is the reason why graphite is useful as the so-called "lead" in pencils.

Diag. 2 - GRAPHITE

In a diamond each atom is joined to four others in a three dimensional pattern. That explains why such a lump of pure carbon is famous as the very hard molecule called diamond.

Diag. 3 - DIAMOND

Despite the fact that those old molecular models were a misrepresentation of reality, they served a useful purpose. They were even used by the chemists, Francis Crick and James Watson, who first worked out the double helical chemical structure of DNA.

The objection, which can be raised against such crude representation of molecular structure, can also be raised against the diagrammatic representation of the association of ideas set out in Diagram 4 below, in which each item in the grid represents an idea. The diagram is intended to represent how each idea is directly associated in the mind with several others, just as one atom of carbon is associated with several other atoms of carbon in a diamond. In representational terms the only difference between associated atoms and associated ideas, is that one atom of carbon is associated with precisely four other atoms of carbon, but an idea may be associated with an indeterminate number of other ideas.

Diag. 4 – GRID OF ASSOCIATED IDEAS

This diagram (and the one on the back cover of this book) is as defective as the molecular models made by chemists a century ago, but it serves a similar purpose. It represents the way in which the electronic records of ideas are associated with each other, like horse & carriage, or love & marriage, but "horse" is also associated with hay & stables & riding. (don't blame me for what you find at the end of that chain of associations. It's your mind.)

Cockney rhyming slang provides good examples of the association of ideas. To a cockney "going up the apples" means going upstairs. In a cockney's mind "apples " are associated with the "pears", which they see on a fruit monger's barrow. That gives "apples & pears". Then pears rhymes with stairs. It may seem absurd, but a cockney's experience of the world creates, in his mind, the association of "apples" with "stairs" via "pears". What ideas associate with each other, depends on every individual's own experience of the world.

When we are busy doing our thinking, the brain checks with electronic speed from one associated idea to the next, until it finds what it wants. If the idea (marked D on the grid at the back of this book) had not been repressed, the brain could check straight across the diagram with lightning speed from idea to idea in order to get from idea A to idea G. That process would be efficient. If, on the other hand, D is put out of bounds by repression, then there is a problem. The obvious result of the ban on the idea at D is that the thought process must make use of other associations, and so go by a circuitous route around D. to get from A to G.

The less obvious result is, that the ideas around D are also out of bounds, because a quick check into one of them might let your thoughts flash on into D by accident. Your subconscious is well aware of that danger. Resistance cuts in, and the chain of associated ideas has to miss out the ideas around X, and go the long way round from A to G.

The use of the circuitous path has two inevitable consequences. One is that the thinking process is slowed down. The other is that the ideas closely associated with D are not available to you as part of your experience of life. They are not available for everyday use in the course of everyday thinking and decision taking

In diagrams 3 and 4 each idea is shown as associated with precisely four others. The traumatic memory, although central to the psycho-neurosis caused by the repression of D, is not necessarily at the centre of your mind, and each idea is not necessarily associated with just four others. Above all, the web must be pictured as three dimensional, to form a sphere of interconnected memories.

There may, of course be more than one repressed trauma, each one surrounded by a clump of ideas, which must stay out of bounds. In that way psycho-neuroses can make the thought process tortuous and cumbersome. They can make thinking slower and less efficient. There is always the danger of stumbling into the traumatic memory, and setting off an emotional cataclysm. The subconscious has been programmed to prevent that happening, and it stands guard over the prohibited associations all day and all night. That explains why people with several psycho-neuroses often feel tired, and are rarely capable of real efficiency or real enjoyment.

Although the diagram on the back cover is only a crude representation of how we think from one idea to the next, it does serve to make the point, that all ideas are either directly or indirectly associated with each other. In the course, of daily conscious thought the associations, which form the chain of ideas, are not "free". They are chosen on the basis of the aim to be achieved. In hypnosis, on the other hand, the subconscious is left to ramble aimlessly through the tangle of ideas associated with each other on the basis of the very personal experience of life. It is allowed to choose "free" as opposed to logical associations. That activity of the subconscious mind in hypnosis is called "Free Association". Properly used in hypnosis or meditation, free association leads to catharsis and consequent cure.

"I realised after $25,000 worth of analysis, that if I'd had that $25,000 in the first place, I would not have needed analysis."

Woody Allen

****

Chapter 11 - FREE ASSOCIATION IN HYPNOSIS

In the face of an experience which seems too awful for you (not necessarily for anyone else) to bear, your defence may kick in, and you may go into denial. You may then set up a program called resistance, which electronically prevents any chain of association from getting near to the memory of that awful experience. Then resistance is in operation, and creates no-go areas around the protected memory. It means that ideas, which happen to be closely associated with the traumatic experience are also put out of use. They are not available for day to day tasks, for taking decisions and for making an invention. That is the sort of block which is illustrated by the two dimensional diagram (diag.6) in chapter 19.

In hypnosis the conscious mind is put to rest. The subconscious is now on its own, and it gets on with the jobs it has to do. It has its longstanding instructions to guard the site of a repressed experience, and to prevent the memory of that experience from being recollected. If that order has not been countermanded, it keeps up the resistance.

Concurrently, the subconscious also knows that the object of the hypnosis, which has left it in sole charge, is to find the repressed memory. That is what its owner wants. The subconscious is now in a quandary. It does not know which way to turn, so it wanders along in a zig-zag path from idea to idea, letting: "I dare not wait upon I would". (If Shakespeare had been a hypno-analyst, he could not have put it better) In consequence the subconscious does neither one thing nor the other, or both at the same time. Ideas, which have no obvious relation to each other, are allowed to associate freely, and the chain of association ultimately leads to the traumatic experience.

The options are now the same as those, which confront anyone with a secret. To keep a secret you have to guard your tongue at all times. You only have to slip up once, and the secret is out. The secret is not a secret any more.

For the subconscious mind in hypno-analysis there is a slight difference. It can allow the hidden traumatic memory to surface. The subconscious can let it be recollected for a second, but resistance has not yet gone away. The secret can submerge again as suddenly as it surfaced. Unless you give immediate voice to that memory, you will find that it is still as elusive as it ever was.

If you voice the memory, you will keep hold of it, because your subconscious knows that the analyst now knows it too - in strictest confidence. If you then discharge the emotion, which caused the trauma to be repressed, or at least describe the feelings which the incident had evoked, the rogue innervation is used up. Then there is nothing left to sustain the symptoms to which the innervation gave rise.

Two more things should be said in this chapter. However long ago the incident occurred, when it is recollected it will seem as if it had happened yesterday. You may even blush now, as you blushed then, or you may jerk now as you jerked then. The memory will then seem very real, but the world has moved on. What seemed an appalling shame, fright, grief or disaster at that time, may now seem ridiculously trivial. It certainly was not worth the affect, which it had on you all those years ago, and continued to have during all those subsequent years.

Time, they say, heals everything. That is true, but only if the idea stays in direct and indirect association with all others. That statement is not true, if the idea was withdrawn from associative contact with other ideas because an effort of denial, and subsequent resistance, locked it away in the hypnoid state. In that case, instead of gaining more experience of life, you have got a block (or a hang-up or worse) from the unfortunate event. That emotional constipation or psycho-neurosis, call it what you like, stays with you. It will stay with you, unchanged, until it is resolved.

****

The term "emotional constipation", intended to mean constipation of the emotions, as an alternative name for psycho-neurosis, should not be confused with physical constipation, which may indeed be a substitute affect from a traumatic experience, and as such itself the symptom of a psycho-neurosis.

Editor

****

Chapter 12 - ANOREXIA

A Case History by David Heard-Smith

I received a phone call for an appointment to discuss the possibility of help for a young woman, 18 years of age, suffering from Anorexia. The client, let's call her Jane, presented herself for the initial consultation accompanied by her mother and twenty year old sister. There was no mention of a father, but that did not seem out of place at this time.

Jane had developed anorexia when she was about thirteen or fourteen years old She seemed a cheerful and well rounded person, but she had periods of intense eating disorder, which played havoc with her health and her life. During the previous five years she had spent long periods in hospital due to the anorexia. At one point she had been close to death, with a body weight of barely five and a half stone (77lb=35kg), and she had only survived by virtue of forced feeding. At that time she also received a certain amount of psychological help, but treatment levels available at that time were rather limited. It had been clear from the outset that the whole family were in need of help, but it was agreed that I should start with the Jane's anorexia.

Jane presented herself for her first session, and at the start she was most cooperative, drifting easily into hypnosis. She appeared to be pleasantly relaxed and at ease. No emotional experience surfaced from her subconscious, and she went away relaxed. Jane duly arrived at the appointed time for her second session, and was very chatty. She reported that she had felt quite good about herself, and appeared keen to proceed. In fact her chattiness was just a manifestation of resistance. She wanted to put off the time when she had to confront her memories. I had a terrible job to persuade her to go onto the couch, and into hypnosis. Eventually we managed to get the session underway, and she proceeded to tell me in 'free association' the ideas, which drifted into her consciousness. However, nothing of importance came to the fore.

The third and forth sessions were much the same as the second and I was becoming a little concerned at the lack of progress. Resistance was still at work, and Jane purported to be feeling a lot better, more relaxed and eating normally. Personally, I was unhappy about those claims, as I didn't believe her. On the other hand I was encouraged by the fact that she had clearly developed signs of transference.

When Jane arrived for the fifth session she was a little sullen and depressed, but after going into hypnosis she very quickly started to relate an experience at the kitchen table. She remembered her mother being present, and that she herself was eating something, when her father entered the room. She then drifted away from that subject, only to return to it a few more times during the remainder of the session. There were no real revelations, but my antenna were twitching. I could tell that she was on the brink of retrieving a significant memory.

In the sixth session Jane very quickly returned to the kitchen table experience, and from what she revealed, her father had been very angry with her. She was a healthy, thirteen year old teenager, and very pretty. In fact, she was her father's 'little princess'. She was, however, inclined to what used to be called 'puppy fat', and very fond of her food, not all of which was necessarily recognised as 'healthy food'. Her father was angry, because she was, 'stuffing her face', and in his anger he said to her: 'How can you expect anyone to love you, when you are so fat. You will make yourself unlovable.' That recollection clearly upset her, but seemingly no more than it would upset any young girl enjoying this kind of relationship with her father.

The sixth session is often climactic, but the experience of the much mentioned kitchen table did not in itself seem significant. Session seven came and went with very little of interest, except for the fact that she had become resistive. This confirmed to me that we had come very close to a crucial revelation in session seven (possibly even in the sixth session) but it is not up to the analyst to speculate on what lies behind seemingly insignificant disclosures.

Session eight started off badly. There was such a lot of resistance to the repressed memory that Jane brought herself out of hypnosis. She even got off the couch, but I persuaded her to try again, and gave her a long induction into hypnosis instead of relying on the quick effect of the post hypnotic suggestion put in place in the first session. Jane calmed down somewhat, went into a good quality hypnotic state, and we again proceeded with recall by "free association".

 Then, very quickly, Jane recalled a situation early one morning, when her mother entered her bedroom and asked her if she had seen her father. Because she said that she had not seen him, her mother asked her to go and find him. She, the mother didn't know where he was, and had to get breakfast ready. Jane searched around the house but to no avail. Eventually she went outside to look in the garden and finally in the garage.

Suddenly all hell was breaking loose with this poor girl! Through her sobs she revealed, that she had opened the garage door, and the first thing she saw, hanging by the neck from a roof beam, was the body of her dear, beloved father. Within seconds, she was abreacting like I had never experience before. All hell broke loose before I had any inkling of what was going on.

I think that she just suddenly saw her father hanging there and burst into tears, throwing herself around with lots of "No, No's" and chewing her fingers and hand, and generally experiencing a great deal of powerful emotion. The thirteen year old child was staring at the dead body of her father, and just "knew" that she had killed him. He had hung himself because she was so fat and unlovable. She had killed her father because she was fat, and he couldn't love her anymore. Well! He would, wouldn't he?

However, as Jane released the emotion of this terrible experience, which she had attributed to her father's angry outburst of the previous day, this brave young woman slowly came to understand the truth of the matter. After ensuring that she was calm, and that she understood the situation, I put her back into hypnosis from which she had again been jolted, and gave her some reassuring suggestions. After such a powerful abreaction I decided not to discharge her from therapy, until it was clear what the next session would reveal.

Session nine started with an explanation from Jane as to what had really happened with her father, and why he had committed suicide. It was clear that his decision to commit suicide had nothing to do with her. I let her carry on talking for a while, and then put her into hypnosis, to let her deal with any anger she might have felt towards her father, or various other people including herself, but that was unnecessary. It was all half hearted, and amounted to nothing more than a sweeping clean of the area of her terrible experiences. Her anorexia was gone. The job had been done the week before, by the effective discharge of her repressed emotions.

In my opinion, nothing other than the cathartic release of those emotions by means of hypno-analysis could have achieved that result. In such cases, orthodox medicine can at best be complementary, because such memories, if repressed, play on the mind. They can not be guessed at, and that internal travail inevitably beats all efforts of external intervention.

I met Jane a couple of years later, and all seemed to be well with her. She definitely appeared happy and content with her life. She had put the terrible experience of her father's suicide behind her.

✱✱✱✱✱✱✱✱

Catharsis brings surprising, liberating enlightenment about yourself, so that you can obey the injunction written on the lintel of the entrance to the temple at Delphi to: "Know Thyself".

Editor

✱✱✱✱✱✱✱✱

Chapter 13 - GUILT (Headaches)

A case history by Heather King

A lady in her mid-forties consulted me about severe headaches, which she had suffered for the last five years. Twelve years earlier she had been in a bad road accident, sustaining serious injuries to her spine, back, shoulders and head, causing headaches. The original treatments were successful, and she had a number of pain free years. Then, suddenly, the headaches reappeared. It was thought that they were a recurrence of injuries sustained in the accident. She revisited the previous therapies at the NHS, chiropractors and osteopaths to no avail.

On the advice of a friend, she consulted me as a last resort. During the initial consultation we established that her mother had died from cancer of the stomach just before the onset of the headaches. We agreed to embark on a course of analytical hypnotherapy. Free association revealed a very loving and supportive family life, with close bonds between my client, her mother and her younger sister. My client was at her mother's side during the last days of her life, and watched her mother clutch her stomach and moan, as painkillers became less effective. The sister, who lived abroad, did not arrive until the last moment. The mother died shortly after the arrival of her younger daughter.

The death of her mother cropped up on a number of occasions, accompanied by some emotional release. The sessions moved between happy childhood memories and the mother's death. During the fifth session that pattern was repeated, until my client became agitated on recalling a previously unvisited occasion when, as a very young, and until then "only" child, she had become angry and frustrated, because her heavily pregnant mother was unable to pick her up. Her mother had explained, that she was carrying a new baby in her stomach, and therefore she could not pick up my client.

In the chair, my client became red-faced and furious at being thwarted. She relived being angry with her mother, and jealous of the new baby who was taking her place. In an absolute rage she had pummelled her mother's stomach, and then ran away screaming to hide from her mother. As she fled, she collided with a wall, banged her head, and passed out. She came around feeling sick and dizzy, surrounded by a crowd including her mother, who was now distraught, gasping for breath, clutching her stomach and crying out: "Oh God, you'll be the death of me." They were both taken to hospital.

When my client was taken home alone by her grandparents, she believed that her mother had died because of her. In the chair my client expressed the extreme guilt and anguish felt at the time on account of that belief, but when her mother came home with the new baby a few days later, her relief enabled her to bury these intense and unresolved emotions.

The trigger to the cathartic release was the memory of her mother clutching her stomach and groaning, as if awaiting the arrival of the "baby" sister immediately prior to death. With the connection between the two events now obvious, my client sat up shouting: "IT WASN'T ME - I DIDN'T DO IT", and burst into floods of tears, fully releasing the unresolved guilt and grief at the supposed earlier death of her mother.

Having now achieved her moment of "surprising, liberating enlightenment" my client opened her eyes and, and with a beaming smile said: " Oh, what a weight off my mind." When she stood up, she realised that, for the first time in five years, the pain in her head had completely gone. I believe that nothing other than the cathartic release through free association in analysis could have achieved that result. This was a typical case in which hypnotherapy was effectively the only therapy. In such a case it is orthodox medicine which could at best be complementary.

****

Obsessions do not have to be bad. An obsession to see justice done is good for society, but it is not good for the individual who has that obsession. It is his prison.
Editor

****

Chapter 14 - CAT PHOBIA

A case study by Anne Priest

Mrs.M. was a lady approaching sixty years of age. She had a husband and three grown-up children. They all of got on very well. The marriage was a happy one. Her parents were both dead, having died when she was in her mid forties. She had been very close to her father, but she had not got on at all with her mother. The mother had told her that she was unwanted, and had abused her as a child. She had an adopted sister, who was five years her senior. My client had got married in her late teens.

There was no history of serious illness, but my client had experienced a phobia of cats since childhood. The phobia was manageable at home, but the lady consulted me because it was preventing her from going abroad to a country, where she had previously encountered a large number of stray cats.

We agreed to embark on a course of analytical hypnotherapy, and we used the retinal fatigue method of induction. Since my client had come for therapy because of her fear of cats, we knew that there had to be a reason for that particular fear. Furthermore, there had to be an incident which was at the root of that fear. By means of the Ideo Motor Response Method (*), of yes and no answers, my client informed me, that such an incident had taken place when she was seven years old. In the incident she was indoors with two male cousins, when something was apparently said which caused her to fear punishment, and she inexplicably developed a fear of cats to avoid such punishment.

My client said that she was prepared to look at the incident in hypnosis. I therefore regressed her to when she was seven years old, and asked her to describe verbally what she saw happening. She said that she saw a black and white cat being carried by a boy, whom she recognised as her cousin. That cat belonged to her grandmother. As the cousin came towards her, he put the cat down, and she felt afraid. Although the boy was fully aware of the fact that she disliked cats, he began chasing the cat towards her. She ran away from the cat, but it was she, who was blamed for being naughty. In consequence she was smacked by her mother.

Using the Ideo Motor Method, my client informed me, that there was another incident involving cats when she was two years old. She saw a black cat moving around, and saw her mother telling her, that if she did not behave, the cat would "get her". Her mother then said that she was very naughty and smacked her. She was forced to sit on a chair, and not allowed to move until she was told.

At this point my client began to sob. That provided the catharsis for the trauma suffered by the two year old child. When my client had calmed down, I arranged another visit one month ahead. During that visit my client told me that, when she left after the last visit her husband drove her home. On getting out of the car, she walked straight past the neighbour's cat without any reaction. In fact her husband had to draw her attention to the fact that she had just ignored the cat. She had several encounters with cats during the month, none of which produced any response in her, and she was now looking forward to her holiday abroad.

We went through the checklist of questions again, but the traumatic incident had been completely resolved, resulting in the total removal of the client's cat phobia.

(*) NOTE ON IDEO MOTOR RESPONSE

That method is sometimes used by therapist to help clients in hypnosis to find the area in which their problem is located.
The therapists asks a series of questions which require only a Yes or No answer., and the clients raise the right forefinger to answer: "Yes", and the left forefinger to answer: "No".

In the fully waking state the clients would not be able to answer those simple questions, but in hypnosis the subconscious mind provides the answers.

A question and answer session with client M might go as follows:-

Therapist: "Did an incident happen before M was ten years old ?
         Right forefinger answers YES.
Therapist: "Did it happen before M was five years old ?
         Left forefinger answers NO.
Therapist: "Did it happen before M was seven years old ?
         Right forefinger answers YES.
Therapist: "At the time of the incident was M indoors ?
         Right forefinger answers YES.
Therapist: "At the time of the incident was M alone ?
         Left forefinger answers NO.

Although a therapist can provide such help to expedite location of the problem, it is still only the client's subconscious mind, which knows where the trouble is seated, and it is still only the client's subconscious mind, which can ultimately locate and recall the traumatic experience.

Chapter 15 - PHOBIA (Fear of Heights)

A case history by Bob Caton

On the instructions of his wife, who was going to book a foreign holiday, a male client reported with a fear of flying. Although he came, expecting the "miracle cure" by means of one session of suggestion therapy, his overall demeanour concerned me. I advised him, that under the circumstances I would not be prepared to offer that kind of therapy, and explained why it would be wrong to do so. I took him through my standard explanation, covering the fact that his fear was the effect of some root cause, and went on to explain how the analysis process worked. He agreed to undertake a process of "free association" analysis. He understood that it was the way in which we could get to, and remove, the root of the problem. He accepted that removal of the cause was better than simply removing the symptoms. That could result in the root cause finding an alternative way to manifest itself.

As is common in the early stages of analysis, the client intellectualised. He attempted to steer the process towards what he considered to be those episodes in his life, which could in his opinion, have contributed to the problem. During this early stage it also came to light, that he experienced mild panic attacks, when in the vicinity of tall buildings. He went on to explain that this problem became more intense if he had to enter a tall building. Any therapist could be excused for believing that there were two separate issues to deal with. What possible link could there be between a fear of flying and being near a tall building?

Once we got over the client's intellectualisation, and his natural desire to be helpful, the process of free association was able to begin. During one of the early sessions a memory resurfaced of the last time that he had flown. (That had already been raised during intellectualisation in session one) It now transpired that during that flight the aircraft hit an air pocket, and dropped some considerable distance. He had been bending forward for some reason so that his head was down, and he was looking towards the floor when it happened. This time we were able to explore his feelings, not just the memory. It soon became apparent to both of us, that it was the act of falling that frightened him, not the actual fact of being in an aircraft and flying.. That in itself came as a revelation to him, and could very easily have been used in suggestion therapy to address the problem originally reported. However, the following events demonstrate why this would have been the wrong thing to do. It would only have dealt with one of the problems, and even that one only partially,

Between session one and session six there was the predictable range of typical memories that, as is usual with this form of therapy, seemed to have no identifiable link or relevance to the problem. Nevertheless, each of those was important in it own right as a stepping stone to the next, which eventually lead us to the ultimate goal. That came to light part way through session six. At about the age of seven the client, in the company of an uncle and two cousins, visited a building, which was regarded as an architectural marvel. It was a wooden church, with a very high steeple, situated somewhere in East Anglia.

Evidently the steeple is open on the inside, and visitors were able to see all the way up the centre, to where the bell hung. To enable visitors to look up into the steeple without craning their necks, a large round mirror had been placed on the floor. Thus visitors were able to look up into the steeple by looking down into the mirror. There was a low rope around the mirror, simply to deter people from walking on it.

While describing this scene, the client became noticeably agitated, and went on to recount how he had walked about, looking up at the high wooden beamed roof, and had then stepped forward to look down into the mirror. At that moment, one of the cousins had come up behind him, and pushed him forward with a jolt, as if to throw him down into the mirror. When recounting that precise moment, the client actually jolted on the couch, and became very distressed.

As therapists we can now clearly see the link between the fear of falling, rather than the fear of flying, and tall buildings. Imagine how tall the building must have seemed to that young mind, and imagine how deep the hole of that steeple must have seemed, when looking down into that mirror.

To those therapists, who are thinking to themselves: "This is not enough. Where is the emotion to cause suppression of the memory?", I say well done! Many of us have had frightening experiences similar to that one, and we simply remember them as incidents that frightened us at the time. After the client had calmed down, it was obvious that he was still very uncomfortable emotionally, and it slowly came out that at the time he had slightly messed his pants with fright. He felt so ashamed and guilty that he did not tell anyone. A classic route to memory suppression!

There remained two months before the client was due to fly on holiday, so we decided to test the situation. He was to visit and enter the highest office block in the town. His subsequent message on my answering machine gave great satisfaction. There had been no problem. As to the fear of flying - I never heard from him again, but I know !

✷✷✷✷✷✷✷✷

"Anybody who goes to see a psychiatrist ought to have his head examined."
Samuel Goldwyn

Chapter 16 - PANIC ATTACKS

A Case History by Iain Dutton

This case involved a young woman twenty-six years of age, whom I shall call Susan. Susan was suffering from panic attacks, and had been on a course of tranquillisers prescribed by her doctor. The case brought home to me the importance of looking for repressed traumas through the process of free association.

Susan's panic attacks began some fourteen months previously, and she thought that she knew the cause. Just before the attacks started, she had been staying with her boyfriend at his flat in London. On her second night, sleeping with her boyfriend, she became aware of the flatmate creeping into the bedroom, and climbing into the bed beside her. She had a lot to drink that night, and she admitted that her resistance had not been as forceful as she would have hoped. Her boyfriend was apparently fast asleep, and was snoring loudly. The flatmate forced himself on her, and finished up by raping her. All the time she had the fear that her boyfriend would wake up, and she was petrified of the consequences.

Next morning, in the cold light of day, Susan became outraged at what had happened, so much so that she decided to tell her boyfriend. His reaction led her to believe that he had not in fact been asleep, and was aware of exactly what had taken place. That was too much for her to cope with, and the next thing she remembered was being interviewed by a police-woman, and having to undergo the trauma of an internal examination. The police decided that there was sufficient evidence to persuade the Crown Prosecution Service to take the case to court.

Susan attended the court case some weeks later. She was already suffering from panic attacks, and she described the ordeal of the trial as "being raped again", but this time in public. As could be expected, her panic attacks became more severe, and it was then that she sought the help of her doctor.

When I first saw Susan it was more than a year after the rape, and her medication had been increased. It seemed to me that she had repressed some of the emotions surrounding the rape and the court case. Therefore I suggested, that the approach we should take would be to release those repressed emotions.

There were indeed plenty of buried feelings that surfaced, and by the fourth session Susan was feeling very much better. The panic attacks had all but disappeared. Under normal circumstances I would have concluded the therapy at this point, but something did not seem quite right. It was nothing I could put my finger on. I just had a sense, that more had to come out. I asked Susan to see me again in a month's time.

By the time Susan turned up for her appointment, she was again suffering from panic attacks. They were not as severe as before. Nevertheless they had got worse again, and I realised that there must be something else needing to be resolved. I explained the process of free association. I asked her to hang her intellect on a hook, to direct her mind into her childhood, and to tell me whatever came into her mind. Three sessions went by with free association, but without apparent progress. Nevertheless I stuck to my belief, and asked her to continue.

When Susan arrived for the fourth session she was in quite an agitated state, but didn't know why. I wasted no time. Within two minutes she was in a deep trance, and recounting incidents from her childhood. Then it came; The moment for which we had been waiting. She found herself very nervous whilst recounting memories of being on holiday with her parents at a caravan site at the age of twelve. She told of going to a disco, and really enjoying herself. She had the notion that she had come home from the disco on her own. It was at this point that she became extremely emotional, and felt that there was a black presence surrounding her. She could feel a great weight on her chest. Gradually, the memory unfolded. She began to realise that on her way back to the caravan a man had grabbed her, and had dragged her behind a hedge and raped her. She remembered that he was a soldier, and that he had threatened to shoot her mother and father, if she were ever to say anything.

Naturally, Susan was somewhat aghast when I brought her out of the trance. It took some time for her to gather her thoughts before leaving. . When she arrived for the next session a week later, I hardly recognised her. She was bright and cheerful, but still somewhat staggered that she could have forgotten such a traumatic event in her childhood. Susan told her parents about what she had uncovered, and they both remembered very clearly how her behaviour had suddenly changed, how she had shut herself away from them, and no matter how much they tried to help her, they just had not been able to get through to her. Her mother had always felt that from the holiday onwards, Susan had changed.

During that short period of a week, Susan had also realised why she had not offered any real resistance when she was raped by the flatmate. She had used the excuse that she had too much to drink, but in fact it was the threat made by the soldier, to which she had been subconsciously reacting. This analysis took place several years ago and it has had the effect of setting in concrete what I have known for some time. Whatever traumas the mind can consciously remember, are effectively dealt with. It is those traumas that have been repressed, and are buried in the subconscious mind, that are at the root of all psycho-neurotic reactions.

Chapter 17 – COMMENTS ON CASE HISTORIES

Although this book mentions therapies, it is not a book about therapy. This book is about three little known facts. It is about the fact that wilful denial or unexpected shock can lock an unacceptable experience away from normal retrieval by the memory. Secondly, this book is about the fact that the innervations from such a repressed idea can cause somatic illness, psychic illness or driven behaviour. Thirdly it is about the fact that any of those afflictions disappears immediately, if the traumatic experience is recalled, and the attached emotion is discharged by overt physical action.

That is the logical order in which to present those three concepts, but they can only be demonstrated in reverse order. If a person, goes into hypnosis with a longstanding stutter, recounts a long forgotten incident of sex abuse as a child, and comes out of hypnosis speaking fluently, you can infer three things. The first is that the stutter disappeared, because the incident was recalled and recounted. The second inference is that the nerve signals from the repressed memory interfered with the nerve signals organising his or her speech. The third inference is that the shock of the abuse prevented him or her from crying, so that the memory was locked away somewhere, where it was inaccessible to everyday thought.

If you have not had all three of such experiences, the only way in which you can get a glimpse of them is at second hand from case histories. To that end, the previous five chapters were case histories, as told by the therapists who helped clients to successful resolution of their psycho-neuroses.

Chapter 12 involves a case of anorexia. The psycho-neurosis was based on a very real and terribly traumatic event, which provided the shock, but the real cause of the anorexia was the imagined guilt. The ferocity of the catharsis showed what powerful emotions had been locked away in the young woman, and had been carried about with her for six painful and dangerous years. The girl always knew that her father was dead, but the traumatic thought was that she was the cause of his suicide. That thought was too much to bear, and was repressed. Innervation from the repressed emotion blocked her ability to eat normally. Recollection of that thought discharged the relevant emotion. The moment of catharsis was clearly visible in this case.

In Chapter 13 the repressed idea was also imaginary. A five year old child believed that she had been the cause of her mother's death. The shock of that thought caused the relevant emotion to be buried in the subconscious. The case also shows that, despite daily contact with her mother over more than thirty years, once the belief had been dissociated from other ideas, it staid intact, in isolation for many years. Innervation from the repressed guilt produced the headaches only after the disaster of the mother's death.

Recollection of the imaginary guilt produced visible catharsis. The emotion was discharged when she shouted out her innocence. Thereafter, the headaches, which no amount of other treatment could cure, were gone.

In Chapter 14 the case history shows how the experience of a very small child may cause a phobia in an adult. The baby's fear of the black cat was buried in the shock of being smacked. The order to sit still prevented any discharge of the baby's feelings at the time, and the undischarged feelings manifested themselves in the adult's fear of cats. That fear disappeared as soon as the traumatic incident was recalled, and the client's sobs discharged the emotion.

In Chapter 15 the therapist was able to identify the moment when fright put the boy into a hypnoid state. The feelings relevant to the incident were buried in the hypnoid state. From there they caused a fear of heights, whenever the man saw a tall building, or thought of going onto an aeroplane. When the exact moment of the traumatic experience was recalled, there was the same physical reaction as the event caused at the time, namely a backward jerk of the muscles of the body. At that moment the relevant emotion was discharged.

In Chapter 16 it is evident from the circumstances of the case, that the victim of a psycho-neurosis may undergo a noticeable change in behaviour. If you have a psycho-neurosis, it turns you into a different person to the one you would have been, if the electronic signals which constitute the psycho-neurosis were not going round and round in your mind. The effect of totality of stress can be seen in this case. The original rape did not cause panic attacks. The addition of the second rape still failed to produce panic attacks. The totality of the hidden stress of two rapes, together with the overt stress of the court case, finally brought on the attacks.

This case history also shows, that one should never guess at the cause of a psycho-neurosis. It is true that the panic attacks started after a well-remembered rape, but the cause of the panic attacks was the earlier "forgotten" rape, which had changed the young woman's behaviour. The shock of the earlier rape had buried the relevant feelings (emotions), and it was the ultimate discharge of those feelings, which stopped the panic attacks, and restored her behaviour to that of her own natural personality.

All those accounts show that, although the victim is aware that there is a problem, no amount of rational thinking enabled the victim to pin down its cause. In all those cases it was the recall of the traumatic experience (real or imaginary) by free association of ideas, which lead to resolution of the problem, and to surprising, liberating, enlightenment. It should not be supposed that the events in every case of psychoneurosis would be readily recognisable as obviously traumatic.

To those five cases, resolved with the help of hypno-analysts, ought to be added the case of catharsis reported in the press in the course of the last decade. The case related to a man who was trapped in his motorcar as a result of a collision. He recalled a previously long forgotten incident of being locked into a cupboard in the course of abuse in his childhood. The car crash evidently put him into the hypnoid state of shock, and the ongoing incarceration enabled him to abreact his childhood trauma. When he got home, his wife perceived, just like the mother of the rape victim, that he was a different (and better) person.

Resolution of a psycho-neurosis brings about a changed thought pattern, because one or more blocks or hang-up have been removed from the mind. The liberated mind is now free to function as it should, with the added benefit of a certain amount of retrieved experience. Inevitably, a changed thought pattern is likely to bring about a changed pattern of behaviour, however subtle. Any such change of behaviour will probably go unnoticed by the world at large. It is the erstwhile neurotic's nearest and dearest, to whom the change of behaviour may be apparent. That change was apparent to the mother of the rape victim in Chapter 16, both immediately after the rape, and again when the consequent psychoneurosis was resolved.

The car case also serves to illustrate the fact that psycho-neuroses or emotional constipation, call it what you will, can be resolved by a life experience. Such a life experience may take place in the course of a real life drama like the car crash. Alternatively, it may take place while comfortably seated in a theatre, if the drama witnessed on the stage portrays a situation analogous to that, which caused the psycho-neurosis.

The events which give rise to a psychoneurosis are often of unbelievable triviality, and would be of importance to nobody except to the person concerned in those particular circumstances, at that particular time. It is another one of the reasons, why nobody can guess at the cause of any particular psycho-neurotic syndrome. (See quotation at end of Chapter 22)

****

"Judge not that ye be not judged"
Matthew Ch, 7 v.1

****

Chapter 18 - TYPES OF THERAPIES

It is true, that a rose by any other name smells just as sweet. It is also true that therapy, by any other name, is just as effective, provided that you choose a therapy which is capable of dealing with your affliction. To make the correct choice you may have to call the relevant therapy by the right name. That brings us hard up against the vocabulary problem, which was already mentioned in the introduction.

People usually use three terms to describe the kind of therapy which they have in mind. Besides orthodox medicine, they talk of complementary and of alternative therapies. Unfortunately, they very often use the terms "alternative" and "complementary" as if they were interchangeable. That is a mistake.

Therapies can properly be called "alternative" if you can arbitrarily choose one in preference to the other, when deciding on treatment for your problem. You can arbitrarily choose to go to an osteopath instead of the doctor, to find out why you can not move your arm after a sporting accident. The doctor or the osteopath may identify the problem. Either of them may deal with the matter for you, or may then send you to the other for treatment. In such a case orthodox medicine and osteopathy may be called alternative therapies.

Complementary therapies have a different function. A therapy can properly be called complementary, if it can be used alongside the main therapy, which treats the cause as well as the symptoms of the problem. You may go to an osteopath to reset a dislocated ankle, and also to a herbalist for a poultice to bring down the swelling. In that case osteopathy is the main therapy, and herbalism offers complementary treatment. Similarly you may go to a hospital for the insertion of a catheter, and call on the services of a hypno-therapist for non-pharmaceutical analgesia. Hypnosis will reduce the pain of that invasive medical procedure, speed up the insertion of the catheter, and reduce the biochemical side effects of the invasion. In such a case, hypnotherapy is complementary to the main procedure, namely the insertion of the catheter.

So far we have discussed the correct use of the terms "complementary" and "alternative" mainly in relation to orthodox medicine, but that is not the whole story. If a patient has a psychosomatic illness, orthodox medicine can not provide a cure. The source of the problem is not in the body. It is not even in the brain. It is in the mind. The problem consists merely of the electronic signals, which constitute the mind. It is a problem of software, not of hardware. Orthodox medicine, which deals with the hardware, can at best be complementary.

If, for example, a patient has a psychosomatic skin condition (a very common phenomenon) no amount of medication, whether internal or external can resolve that problem. Medication will at best ameliorate the condition. The problem can only be resolved by finding the repressed memory, which is the source of the irritating innervation causing inflammation of the skin. In such cases, psycho-therapy has to be the main therapy. A complementary therapy may provide an ointment to soothe the skin, while analytical hypno-therapy takes it is course, and cures the problem. The complementary therapy gives the patient time find the cause of the problem by means of psycho-therapy, but it can not provide an alternative to the psycho-therapy.

In cases of psychic paralyses, the distinction between therapies is even more obvious. If a traumatic experience causes the mind to block the movement of certain muscles, the paralysis can only be cured by removing the mental block. In such a case orthodox medicine can be neither complementary nor alternative to psycho-therapy. In such cases psycho-therapy is the only remedy.

Psycho-therapy might take the form of religious absolution from guilt. It may take the form of some enlightening experience in real life, or in a drama watched on stage. It can take any form, which makes the old trauma seem acceptable in the light of present day experience, but those are all chance events. The most obvious and most reliable form of psycho-therapy, the most reliable way to reach the problem hidden in the mind, is analytical hypno-therapy. That lets the paralysed patient find his own way to the site of the repressed memory, which is causing the paralysis. That enables him or her to discharge the trauma. The patient is in charge. The hypno-analyst is largely a bystander.

It is important to realise that there are two forms of hypno-therapy, namely suggestion therapy and analysis. In suggestion therapy the hypnotist puts ideas into the patient's mind. That can be very useful to avoid unnecessary pain during dentistry or surgery, but its effect is usually short term. In hypno-analysis the hypnotist allows the client to rummage in his own mind, and to find the cause of the problem for himself. When the cause of the problem is remembered, the relevant emotion can be discharged or described. Then the affect which the traumatic memory produced is gone, but nothing has been put into the patient's mind. The patient's mind is now his own again, as it was before the trauma took it over.

The kind of excessive, wanton shopping, which is often referred to as retail therapy, is not a form of psycho-therapy. It is, however, probably an outward sign of a psycho-neurosis.

****

"Don't adjust your mind. There's a fault in reality."
Anonymous

****

Chapter 19 - FORGETTING (Resistance at work)

At one time Freud toyed with the idea of a "Project for a Scientific Psychology". That project came to nothing, but Freud had earlier written a paper on how we forget. In that paper Freud related how, on a journey from Ragusa to a town nearby, he had related to his travelling companion what he had been told by a medical colleague. That doctor had practiced among the population of the Austro-Hungarian province of Bosnia-Hercegovina for many years. He had said that the local people respected their doctors. If a relative died in their care, they would politely say "Herr, I know that if anything could have been done, you would have done it". The doctor's other story had related to sexuality, in respect of which the local men took the view, that if their sexual capacity failed, life was not worth living.

Later, when the conversation on Freud's journey turned to Italian art, he found to his great frustration, that he could not remember the name of the painter "Signorelli". That frustration staid with Freud for some days, until someone else reminded him of the missing name.

All the above ideas had been associated in his mind. The name Signorelli, which begins with the Italian word for Herr (ie Sir) would have reminded him of the unwelcome news of the death of his own patient, received in Trafoi. In consequence his association of ideas was deflected to other similar ideas.
To explain this experience he drew the quasi scientific diagram set out below.

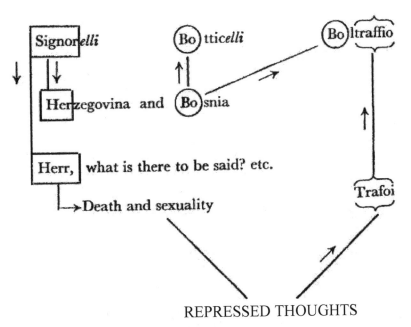

REPRESSED THOUGHTS

The repressed thought was the news received in the town Trafoi of the death of a patient from a sexual disease.

Diag. 5 - HIS DIAGRAM

Freud's diagram is useful, because it shows the memory's attempts to come up with the correct answer are deflected to something else, in order to avoid blundering by association into the core of the memory which his subconscious mind wanted to avoid. In that way the diagram does, indeed, serve to illustrate the process at work when we "forget" (or rather, are unable to remember) but from the point of view of this book it illustrates two other processes.

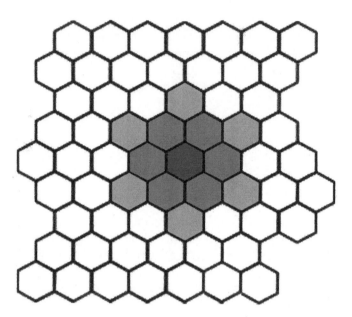

Diag. 6 – SHOWING BLACK TRAUMA IN NO-GO AREA

In effect the diagram shows how the traumatic spot, shown above in black, and its surrounding barrier of defences impedes and deflects the path of everyday practical thinking. That makes thinking less efficient. Secondly it illustrates the barrier, which has to be traversed, in order to reach the traumatic spot itself, and achieve recall on the way to possible catharsis.

This diagram and the one on the back cover show the process of free association of ideas at work, (a) when it approaches the barrier and refuses to go in, (b) when it skirts the barrier to reach its goal by another route, and (c) when it wanders around among the associated ideas until, in hypnosis, it finally gets to the traumatic spot.

One picture is worth a thousand words
Chinese Proverb

✱✱✱✱✱✱✱✱

Chapter 20 - SIGMUND FREUD

Some people think that the best place to begin a subject, is at the beginning. In the case of psycho-neuroses the beginning is in the book called "Studies on Hysteria".

Freud had a lot to say on the subject of the human mind and nervous system. There are fifteen volumes of The Standard Edition of the Collected Psychological Works of Sigmund Freud. The Studies on Hysteria are a part of that collection. It is one of the claims made in the collection, that even the fifteen volumes do not contain all of Freud's utterances.

Some of what Freud said in those volumes and elsewhere was mistake. He often said so, but that does not impugn catharsis. The resolution of hysteria (nowadays regarded as psycho-somatic illness) by means of hypno-analysis was first noted and understood by Breuer, who passed his discovery on to Freud. The validity of that assertion appears clearly enough from Freud's obituary of his mentor. In that tribute Freud wrote, that his own chief merit in connection with the Studies on Hysteria lay in having persuaded Breuer to agree to their publication.

Three quotations from the text of the Studies themselves seem to put the matter beyond doubt. *"It is very hard"* Freud wrote *"to obtain a clear view of neurosis, before one has submitted it to a thorough analysis --- an analysis which can in fact only be brought about by Breuer's method."*

A little further on in the text Freud added: *"On another occasion again, I tried to apply Breuer's method to the treatment of neuroses which no-one could have mistaken for hysteria,* (i.e. which were not psycho-<u>somatic</u> afflictions, but were paranoia or obsession) *and I found that in that manner they (too) could be influenced, and indeed cleared up."*

Finally Freud illuminated the reason why he developed PSYCHO-analysis to replace HYPNO-analysis as a road to catharsis. He wrote: *"When I attempted to apply to a relatively large number of patients Breuer's method of treating hysterical symptoms by an investigation and abreaction under hypnosis, I came up against difficulties, in the course of which I was lead to an alteration both of my technique and to my view of the facts."*

Freud had found that not all his clients could be hypnotised by him. He thereupon replaced the Talking Cure, nowadays called Hypno-analysis, with Psycho-analysis. He used the word "analysis" because he was trying to find out how his patients' minds worked. The word analysis was then inadvertently carried forward, when the talking cure came to be called hypno-analysis. Freud also discovered that Catharsis applies to case of obsession, phobias and paranoia as well as in cases of hysteria. i.e. psycho-somatic illness.

Later, in an autobiographical study, written in 1925, Freud confirmed his generous tributes to Josef Breuer in the clearest possible terms: *"If the account I have given so far has lead the reader to expect that the Studies on Hysteria must, in all essentials of their material content, be the product of Breuer's mind, that is precisely what I have myself always maintained."*

Nowadays, the value of Freud's work included in the fifteen volumes of his published writings, is a matter of (usually ill-informed) opinion. Unfortunately, much of it is currently subject to such general dispute, that the phrase "Freud Bashing" has become common currency in the English language.

Personal attacks apart, Freud's work covers so many aspects of psychology that it is relatively easy to find fault with his work and views, but catharsis (by whatever name) is not a matter of opinion. Catharsis is clearly demonstrated in the five case histories related by five separate practitioners in chapters 12 to 16 of this book, just as it was in the five cases recorded in the Studies on Hysteria.

Freud was really a neurologist, whose province was nervous system in the human body, but his contribution to psychology of the human mind can not be denied.

****

"Freud is the father of psycho-analysis. It has no "mother"
Germaine Greer

The Lady is mistaken. Josef Breuer was the father of psycho-analysis. Freud performed the function of its mother.
Editor

****

Chapter 21 - JOSEF BREUER

The reason for bringing up the subject of "Breuer's mind" (as Freud put it) is that Breuer not only showed how psycho-neuroses could be cured. He also pointed out how psycho-neuroses are contracted.

In 1893, when Josef Breuer and Sigmund Freud published the "Preliminary Communications" about their forthcoming book, to be called "Studies on Hysteria" they jointly expressed the opinion that the basis and *sine qua non* of hysteria is the existence of hypnoid states. In the subsequent book, published in 1895, they jointly revealed how psychoneuroses can be identified, and indeed cleared up, but they each made a separate theoretical contribution to that epoch making volume.

When it came to the causes of hysterias, with which Breuer and Freud were concerned, Freud went down a route of his own. Breuer stuck to his original view, saying: "I am still of the opinion that hypnoid states (such as daydreams) are the cause and necessary condition of many, indeed of most, complex hysterias.

In making that assertion in 1895, Breuer did not fail to point out that P.J. Moebius had, as early as 1890 drawn attention to some of the aspects of hypnoid states in the aetiology of hysterias.(*) Breuer went on to say that fright and anger, as well as exhausting factors such as sleeplessness and hunger, are among the causes of the hypnoid states in which psycho-neuroses can develop.

The examples given by Breuer are only a small proportion of the situations in which hypnoid states develop. They have all been identified by the public, and have given rise to a range of everyday words and phrases. Some examples of such words and phrases are "stunned", " banjaxed", and "speechless" as well as "rooted to the spot" and "paralysed with fear".

Words and phrases can, of course be abused by being employed to colour language, or for the purpose of exaggeration, but when properly used to describe an overwhelming situation, they speak of the sort of hypnoid state in which a psycho-neurosis can develop.

(*) See also Delboeuf and Binet in Chapter 29

"To avoid delay, please have all your symptoms ready"
Notice in a surgery

Chapter 22 - THE DIGITAL WATCH ANALOGY

In 1895 Dr.Josef Breuer tentatively suggested an analogy between electric currents and nerve impulses. Today we know that those nerve impulses can be measured in millivolts. In Breuer's time electricity was a novelty in the houses of the wealthy, and when Breuer wrote about hypnoid states and "splitting of the mind", he did not know about computers and digital watches.

We, however, have always known, that there are at least three states in the human mind, the waking state, a hypnoid state between waking and sleeping, and the sleeping state, but we do not have to call them "states". We can just as well call them modes. If we do that, everything becomes clear to those who are familiar with the modes of digital watches

Nowadays, more than a century after the publication of the Studies on Hysteria, we know all about the "programs" of computers and the "modes" of digital wrist watches. A modern watch has at least two modes. One of those is the wide awake mode, in which the watch tells us the time. The other would be the quasi hypnoid state, called the alarm mode. To make use of two such modes in a digital watch, there are three buttons

If you press a certain one of those three buttons, the watch goes out of time announcing mode, and goes into alarm mode. Then you can not see the time, but "subconsciously" the watch still keeps time.

By pressing the correct buttons you can now set the time of the alarm, advance the time when the alarm goes off, or retard it. We can also turn the alarm on or off, but while the watch is in alarm mode, those same buttons can do nothing at all to the time keeping function of the watch.

Just as nothing you can do with those buttons can do anything to the timekeeping function of the watch, while it is in alarm mode, so nothing you can do with those buttons can change anything in the alarm function of the watch, while it is in timekeeping mode. The relationship between our waking mode and our hypnoid mode is similar.

Laying aside the fact that we can switch much more easily between waking mode and hypnoid mode, than a watch can be switched between timekeeping mode and alarm mode, it explains why a person, who has acquired a psycho-somatic illness (neurosis) in a hypnoid state, has to go back into a hypnoid state to get rid of that psycho-somatic illness. The same thing can, of course, be said of other varieties of psycho-neuroses, like phobias and behavioural aberrations.

List of Colloquial Terms referring to the Hypnoid Mode brought about by "SHOCK"

Aghast
Appalled
Banjaxed
Catching your breath
Fright
Gasped
Gob smacked
Jaw dropped
Open mouthed
Overcome
Overwhelmed
Rooted to the spot
Shocked
Scared stiff
Slapped in the face
Speechless
Stunned
Stagestruck
Thunderstruck

List of Colloquial Terms referring to the Hypnoid Mode into which you can just Drift

Absence
Alpha rhythm
Day dream
Dwam (Scottish term)
Enthralled
Meditation
Reverie
Self hypnosis
Vacancy
Wandered
Wishful thinking
Wool gathering

****

"Here I may remark in passing, that Breuer's view of the origin of hysterical symptoms is not shaken by the discovery of traumatic scenes which correspond to experiences that are insignificant in themselves. For Breuer assumed – following Charcot – that even an innocuous experience can be heightened into a trauma, and can develop determining force, if it happens to the subject when he is in a special psychical condition – in what is described as a hypnoid state."
Sigmund Freud – The Aetiology of Hysteria

Chapter 23 - AN ALARMING HABIT

At the very outset of the disclosure of their discovery of catharsis, Breuer and Freud recorded the scientific observation, than mere recollection of an experience, without the relevant affect, almost invariably produces no result. (i.e.no improvement in the person's condition). The same is true of digital watches. Once you have gone into alarm mode, and set a digital watch, it has the alarming habit of "going off" at the set time day after day, whether or not you want it to do that. What can you do to cure it of that "habit" ?

You can put the watch back into alarm mode. The watch will duly "recollect" the details of its setting. If you then just take the watch back into its normal time keeping mode, nothing else will change. The mere recollection of the time set in alarm mode will have had no effect. Its alarming habit will continue.

To "cure" the watch of its digital alarm "neurosis", you have to go into alarm mode, and do something. In the case of a digital watch, that something is the pressing of a button to discharge the alarm function (i.e. press a button to choose the "disable alarm" option). That is to say, that more than recollection of the alarm setting is required. A specific action is needed to prevent the alarm from going off in the future. If you chose the "disable alarm" option, the alarm will still remember the details of the setting, but it will not go off in the future

In the same way, an overt action has to be performed in the hypnoid mode, in order to stop a neurosis from triggering (on future occasions) the affect, (e.g. paralysis, phobia or behavioural quirk, *et al.*) which it has triggered in the past. That specific overt action, whether it is weeping, laughing, shuddering, or talking about it, serves as an acknowledgement of the emotional impact of the relevant event. The overt action can take other forms of emotional discharge, such as shouting, raging or puffing. It can simply take the form of a detailed verbal description, or written account, of the relevant traumatic experience.

There is an important difference between the alarm function of the watch and the neurosis of the mind. The alarm function of the watch can be re-activated, but once the neurosis has been discharged it is gone. That is good for the patient, but it is bad for science, because the neurosis and its catharsis can not be repeated for demonstration purposes during one of the lectures at the Royal Society. (See Chapter 43 on research)

"Know Thyself"
On the lintel above the entrance to the Temple at Delphi.

Chapter 24 - YOUR OWN MIND

This book does not aim to be about therapy. It is about a problem, without claiming to be about the solution to that problem. The solution to the problem may be psycho-therapy, but therapy is a matter for an outside agency.

Conversely, your mind is your own. It is up to you, what you do with your own mind, once you know how it works. The equivalent of pressing the right button to stop the wrist watch from persisting in its "alarming habit" is to give overt physical expression to the recollection of your traumatic experience.

It may be that on several occasions, when you happened to drift into a hypnoid state, you recollected an uncomfortable experience. If you simply allowed the memory to return into the depths of your subconscious mind, the affect which it has had on you in the past, will have continued. If you wish to be rid of the relevant affect, you need to seize the moment. You need to switch the alarm off. That is called abreaction, and it will produce catharsis.

If you give overt physical expression to your recollection of a trauma, thereby acknowledging how you really felt about that experience, the alarming habit can be switched off. The affect which it had on you in the past, will be gone. That can be done by speaking about it out loud, or by crying, raging or trembling,

There are, however, two important differences between you and the digital watch. Whereas the alarm can be reactivated by going into alarm mode, and switching the alarm on again, you can not go back into hypnoid mode, and switch the affliction on again. Once the affliction has gone, it has gone, and you might indeed say "gone for good".

The other difference between you and the watch is equally important. Whereas the watch can not recollect the alarm setting in the timekeeping mode, you will now be able to recall the traumatic incident at will, and at any time. That means that you have now accepted it. You are no longer in denial. The event has become part of your learning experience. You will have achieved "surprising liberating enlightenment", and the experience will be available to you for use at any time, when steering your way through life.

✱✱✱✱✱✱✱✱

In this book there is a certain amount of repetition, because the subject of this book is like a diamond. It has many facets. It is the facets, that make a diamond.
Editor

Chapter 25 - WILLPOWER

Two very different sorts of experience need to be discussed in relation to willpower. The simpler situation is the one in which the experience leaves no visible trace by which it can be remembered. Either the person was already in hypnoid mode, when the traumatic experience was perceived, or shock took his or her breath away, and put the victim into a hypnoid mode. In that state no emotional discharge takes place, and the experience is neither seen, nor remembered in the waking mode. From there, the psychoneurosis wreaks its havoc in the form of one or more affects, without the victim having any idea of the cause of the problem.

Alternatively, the effect of the traumatic experience may be all too evident, while the way in which the individual was affected by it may be obscure. The death of a member of the family, or the loss of a limb, would be two brutal examples of such a situation. In such a case the experience may be instantly understood, so that the victim cries or screams. In that case the painful emotion connected with the incident is discharged.
.

If, on the other hand, the victim of the traumatic experience perceives what the experience implies, and metaphorically shouts "oh nooh!! – No, no, not that", or alternatively "I do not believe it. That isn't me", then victim has opted for denial or dissociation. Then willpower is resisting the reality. They have opted for wishful thinking. In effect they have opted for a daydream, and daydreams are a hypnoid mode.

Logically there should be no scope for denial. The loved one is missing from the dinner table. The lost limb is all too visible by its absence, but what is lost in the denial, the daydream, the hypnoid mode, is not the starkly obvious reality, but the affect which the experience should logically have had on the victim. The starkly obvious reality can not be switched off, but the affect on the victim can be switched into denial or dissociation by willpower.

There is a price to pay for that effort of willpower. The innervation, which should have found an outlet in emotional discharge, is trapped in emotional constipation. It can become a full-blown psycho-neurosis, which may amount to a psycho-somatic illness. In that case the innervation has been driven out of the mind into the body. That can genuinely be called a *tour de force*, and it explains why people with a serious psycho-neurosis usually manifest (and admit to having) a strong will.

The denial, into which willpower can put the mind, by instantaneously switching into the hypnoid mode, is difficult to maintain in the face of the physical consequences of the event. Then willpower again comes into play, to prevent the emotion from bursting out of the hypnoid state. Tears have to be choked back by willpower, and the damage done by the original flight from reality is thus consolidated.

If the somatic (i.e. physical) demands of hunger, thirst and sexuality of a vertebrate creature have been met, its nervous system likes to be at rest. An antelope likes to lie down quietly chewing the cud. A well fed lion is happiest lying lazily in the sunshine. Horses like to stand quietly, head to tail with another horse, swishing their tails to keep the flies off the other horses face. A man likes to sit in the shade watching the float on his fishing line drifting gently on the water. In such situations of perfect bliss there is no untoward excitement in the nervous system. (provided of course, that there is no underlying psycho-neurosis).

If an alarming situation suddenly arises, if a leopard appears unexpectedly out of the undergrowth, antelope, horse, man and even the lion would get alarmed. Excitation would run riot in the nervous system, especially if the situation turns out to be traumatic. That available innervation can be discharged by flight or by fight, by shouting or waving the arms, or by an emotional discharge like rage or tears. It is easy to see that, if the reaction is to freeze in fright, then the available excitation has to go somewhere. Thus, if you freeze in fright, it becomes a loose cannon. It can and it will produce unpredictable mischief.

That hypothesis is all very well, when the psychoneurotic affect is immediate and finite. It is less easy to understand if the affect is neither immediate nor finite. It is even more difficult to understand, if the affect is intermittent, and the patient has intermittent symptoms or the individual has (intermittent) moods.

In intermittent cases the problem would seem to be even greater than in perpetual cases, but that is an illusion. The fact is that the troublesome thoughts are always trying to rise to the surface, but resistance is at work, keeping them temporarily at bay. Originally, fear triggered the energy for fight or flight. When, for some reason, a quiescent memory threatens to break out, fear again provides the energy for fight or flight, and hence for the symptoms of the psycho-neurosis, which is the substitute for the fight or flight that did not take place. If that happens then the effect of the attack (i.e. the effect of the psycho-neurotic affect) is that the mind is distracted from any chain of association which would lead to the traumatic experience, from which the attack originally sprang.

The above phrase, pointing out the "effect of the affect" brings us back to the importance of the difference between those two words, back to G.K.Chesterton and back to the archetypal Yorkshireman, whom we met in the first chapter. It brings us back to the unreasonableness of the world, and to the queerness of folk. In short it brings us back to the illogicality of the whole subject of psycho-neuroses. But from there we must move forward to the difference between the questions of "why" and "how". The natural sciences are logical. If you want to investigate a phenomenon, you have to ask "How?" You have to ask: "How does this happen?" You have to investigate how the cause relates to the effect, but psycho-neuroses are different. They are illogical. You have to ask: "Why does this happen?" The answer is constipation of the emotional response. The answer is that an emotion has intervened. If that emotion is not discharged you are left with the emotional constipation called psycho-neurosis.

That seemingly pedantic point is of the utmost importance. It is fundamental to the subject of psycho-neuroses. If you take a case of psycho-neurosis to a doctor of medicine (who is in essence a natural scientist) he will be well aware of how the body should normally function. He will know the details of that functioning, or he can look them up in a book of physiology. All the steps in the process will be logical, and he can describe them.

FOR EXAMPLE :- After doing tests, a doctor may be able to tell you that *"your pain is due to "Neurogenic Inflammation". Stimulation of C fibres is causing a local reaction consisting of vasodilatation and increased capillary permeability. This is due to retrograde transport and local release of sP and calcitonin gene-related peptide. As a consequence, K+, H+, acetylcholine, histamine and bradykinin may be released, and these in turn cause prostaglandin and leukotriene production (which may end up sensitizing high-threshold mechanoreceptors)! Neurogenic inflammation may spread to surrounding tissues antidromically."*

With such scientific data the doctor is able to give the patient a complete explanation of "HOW" he or she comes to have pain from an inflamed joint in the left knee. The doctor will then try to intervene physically in the deviant process, which he has described. The patient will be impressed by the totally accurate explanation, and grateful for the physiological intervention. Equipped with that perfectly correct information, the doctor would seem to be in complete control of the situation, if it were not for the awkward customer - a patient with two left feet - who says: "Thank you doctor, I understand the sequence of events which are scientifically taking place, but I want to know: 'Why?' - I want to know WHY all that is taking place? Why ? Why ? Why ? The answer is that an emotion intervened. The effect of such emotions is that the human mind overrides the normal physiological functioning of the body.

All the steps in the process of an affliction are cause and effect, but WHY is that process taking place at all? Is there a cause, which is not producing effect, but is producing affect? Is there an emotional cause, which does not show up in the doctors test tube, or under the doctors microscope? Is it a case of emotional constipation, which is totally illogical, as emotions usually are? Is it simply a case of illogical affect (repressed emotions) which are setting off a chain of completely logical deviant effects in the body's physiology? How can you tell? How can the doctor tell? How can anyone tell?

There are various psycho-therapeutic methods which can cure such psycho-neuroses, but there are only two methods by which you can hope to tell why the patient has that affliction. One method is psycho-analysis, as practised by Freud, and the other is what Freud called "Breuer's method", nowadays called hypno-analysis. Both those methods rely on the patients disclosing the circumstances, which illogically caused them to get the afflictions bringing them to the surgery. Only the patient knows what happened, and only the patient can know "why" he or she got that troublesome "affect". Sooner or later, someone will have to tell the medical profession that their patients have minds subject to emotions, and that the minds are actually attached to the bodies the doctors have to treat.

Chapter 27 - HOMOSEXUALITY

If you have understood the preceding chapters of this book, you will be well aware, that a psychoneurosis can produce any manifestation of which the human body and the human mind are capable. It can certainly simulate the symptoms of well recognised somatic (physical illnesses.

You will also know that no amount of determination can overcome the symptoms of the particular affect, which the loose innervation from a repressed emotion has chosen as its outlet in any individual case. You can not force yourself to eat properly if you have anorexia. You can not force yourself to walk, if you have a psychic paralysis of the legs. You can not force yourself to abstain from gambling, if you have a gambling obsession. You can not "bring yourself" to touch a cat, if you have a genuine cat phobia (as opposed to a mere aversion). So what would happen, if a healthy man had a woman phobia, or a healthy woman had a man phobia?

This is not a subject for the kind of "Instant Think", which is so popular today. It is a serious question, which requires deep thought. Ever since homosexuality has become politically correct, there has been much speculation about its causes. A few intrepid souls have even raised the question of whether people can be "cured" of it. Some people think that homosexuality is innate. Others think that it is due to external factors. On one side of the debate, Jung thought that it was a manifestation of incomplete maturity, due to lack of adequate male guidance. On the other side of the debate, those who say that it is inbred, fail to tell us whether it is in the genes, or due to nurture in the womb. Now a statistical scientist even claims to have found, that the incidence of homosexuality seems to vary with the position of the individual in the sibling row. From that statistic he is reported to have speculated that the sequence of pregnancies produces changes in the womb, which lead to the development of homosexuality in the offspring.

I do not know who is right, or what evidence the various protagonists have for their respective views. The evidence we do all have, is that all animals, including *homo sapiens* have primeval urges. One of those urges is to have sex, but that is not the only primeval urge. There is also the inbred urge to eat, and the urge to drink. They are not psychic urges. They are all somatic urges. A young partridge chick straight out of the egg does not get fed. It has to run with the family, and feed itself. It has to eat. If it does not have the natural urge to eat, it will not live long.

Young antelopes are wary of lions, but in a drought they brave the lion beleaguered waterholes. Nobody has taught them that they must drink. They have a primeval urge to drink. Their urge to drink is stronger than their fear of lions. Any antelope, that does not have the irresistible urge to drink, will soon die of dehydration, even in the shade.

A young male fox normally has the urge to eat and the urge to drink. He also has an inherent urge to have sex. That latent urge is known as sexuality.

The young male fox has sexuality, but he does not get lessons in sex. If he meets a vixen on heat, he just gets the urge to mate. He does not know why, or how, to do that. He just does it. Any male fox that does not have the urge to mate is the dead end of his line. Without an inborn urge to mate, foxes would soon die out. The urge to eat, the urge to drink and the urge to mate are fundamental. They have to be inbred into the gene pool of the species. The lack of that drive would inevitably bring about the end of any species that is without it. Not even a creationist can deny that fact.

All three of those urges are fundamentally the same. They are all somatic. They are all in the body, and not in the mind, but there is one conspicuous difference between them. Individuals, that do not eat, or do not drink, do not live long. They disappear very quickly from the face of the earth.

Things are very different with the urge to mate. An individual without the urge to mate can be around for a very long time. A Galapagos tortoise or a man without the urge to mate may live for a hundred years. However long they may survive, individuals of whatever species, that do not have the urge to mate, do not concern us in this chapter. They will not mate, and they will not exhibit any tendency to homosexuality either.

To discover the why and wherefore of homosexuality, we need only discuss the position of individuals who do have that primeval sexual urge, or "sex drive". Those individuals are indeed driven, and if that drive can be fulfilled, they will fulfill it. Under normal circumstances they will seek, and they will find, the means to fulfill it - namely a member of the opposite sex. So what happens if that sex drive is thwarted ?

Since nobody seems able to tell us the answer, we have to work it out for ourselves, as best we can. With that problem in mind, we could turn for intellectual guidance to the nearest available gurus, our neighborhood farmer's docile cows. Our newfound gurus are all perfectly respectable members of their herd, until they suddenly get the urge to mate. If they were in the wild, they would just sidle up to the nearest mature bull, and that would soon be that.

For dairy cows that is not so easy. Dairy herds are locked into fields, imprisoned by barbed wire fences and five-barred gates. Our gurus, who are normally models of feminine bovine behaviour, can see no way out. They must have sex, or they will get a somatic neurosis. They do not know that. It is not a psychic matter. They just feel it in their muscles, and so to speak "in their bones".

The primeval urges in their bodies tell them that they must have sex, but they cannot get to a bull. So what is going to happen ? They get lesbian tendencies, and leap onto the back of other cows. In agricultural terms they start "bulling". Steel wire and solid wooden gates prevent them from getting the chance of normal sex, so they turn to the next best thing.

That predicament of our bulling gurus should set us thinking. "What if" we can ask ourselves (but not without due circumspection*) "male or female individuals were to encounter obstacles, less visible than barbed wire, and stronger than five-barred gates?" Would their sex drive then soak away into the sand ?

If I were not a hypno-analyst, familiar with psychoneuroses like obsessions, phobias and paranoia the question of obstacles stronger than wood and steel might well puzzle me. For a hypno-analyst, however, that question poses no serious problem. Every hypno-analyst knows, how utterly hogtied any individual may be, if he or she happens to be in the grip of a repressed experience, causing a psycho-neurosis.

I might almost be tempted to think: "What if somewhere, there were a perfectly normal person, who has a perfectly normal psycho-neurosis, the affect of which creates such an invisible barrier, keeping him or her from the opposite sex?" What if a man were to have a woman phobia ? Dare I ask, how the position would be different from that of a fenced-in cow ?

What would be the options for such a person ? How would he, or she, know that there were such options ? How could they find out whether they have such a psycho-neurosis - say such a phobia ?

Those questions have never been raised in public, but when in doubt consult the oracle at Delphi. Even before you go into the temple, the inscription above the lintel adjures you to "Know Thyself". Then the only way to follow its injunction is to rummage in your subconscious mind. You can do that in meditation, or in self hypnosis. Alternatively, you can invoke the aid of a hypno-analyst, who will help you to rummage. Nobody knows what is in your mind, and even you are not sure. The only way in which you will find out what is concealed in your subconscious mind, is by what Freud called "Breuer's method".

All I can say is that there are reported cases, where men sought the help of hypno-analysts for some unrelated presentation symptom, and ceased to be gay after their psycho-neuroses were discharged.

*Circumspection is needed, because strong emotions are involved in the subject of homosexuality. Some of those emotions are self-evident, but other emotions aroused in the course of discussions of this subject, may be of the same sort of run-of-the-mill, repressed emotions, which this book seeks to address.

Chapter 28 - INFERTILITY

Infertility is an emotive subject, and fertility treatment is an expensive business. Now we are told (Aberdeen University 08.08.08) that infertile couples, who have no identifiable biological defect, are just as likely to conceive without treatment as they are with treatment. That is baffling, but it is not inexplicable. It tells us that such infertility is probably psycho-somatic. Prior to the Studies on Hysteria published by Breuer and Freud all neuroses were lumped together. The treatment of Bertha Pappenheim, published in the Studies on Hysteria under the name Anna O. lead to the realisation that there were two very distinct kinds of neuroses, namely organic neuroses and psycho-neuroses.

Whether or not a neurosis is psychic can, as Freud put it: "only be established by Breuer's method". That statement is not strictly correct. Freud himself wrote a paper on the distinctions between psychic and organic paralyses, by which some psychic paralyses can be identified. Furthermore, the symptoms of a psycho-neurosis may be similar to the symptoms of a known organic illness. The psychic nature of an affliction can be inferred, if the medication prescribed for the organic illness, disconcertingly has absolutely no effect on the symptoms. That phenomenon should not be a surprise. If the problem is in the mind, there is no point in pressing buttons in the body.

The same explanation, namely that there is no point in seeking in the body, solutions to problems which are in the mind, applies to infertility in couples without a biological defect between them. The fact that the infertility treatment, which should result in conception (that includes the "treatment" called intercourse) fails to produce pregnancy in an otherwise healthy couple, is a sure indication, that the infertility is psychosomatic. That diagnosis is confirmed by the fact that such infertility can resolve itself spontaneously. Like all psycho-neuroses, it can "wear away", or be resolved by a specific life experience, which has some relevant psychological meaning to that individual. Adoption, for example, is frequently followed by pregnancy in previously barren women.

Acceptance of the fact that infertility in otherwise healthy couples may be psychosomatic, leads to two conclusions. The negative conclusion is that there is no point in trying to find solutions to that infertility in the body. There is no point in digging for truffles where none exist. The positive conclusion is that the solution to psychic infertility can be found by "Breuer's method", that is to say by the method Dr.Josef Breuer used in the treatment of Bertha Pappenheim, namely hypno-analysis. It can also be cured by any other method (say drama therapy) which is capable of discharging the infertile individual's own particular repressed traumatic experience.

One might add, that any individual freed of his or her particular hang-ups, (or queerness as our Yorkshire friend would have put it) will in any case be a better parent than he or she might otherwise have been.

Chapter 29 - SOCIAL CONTEXT

This is another difficult chapter. Who wants to read about babies' piss and babies' pooh? Nevertheless, little children have to learn how to cope with those frequent phenomena. They also have to learn how to deal with their emotions. Those are the three dreadful "P"s (piddle, pooh and paddy), with which babies have to learn to cope. Although social circumstances sometimes demand that the first two of them have to be held back, they must be disposed of sometime, in fact as soon as possible. They must be discharged - but not in public.

The same should be said of the third monster, namely paddies, but that is not what happens. Children are not encouraged to release their emotions. Children are trained to choke their emotions back, but paddies are just like piddle and pooh. They must be discharged, but preferably not in public.

All our training goes against releasing our emotions. Hence, when a catastrophe strikes, there is a split second of doubt – cry out, or choke back? In that split second of time the victim of the catastrophe may go into a hypnoid state, in which the drama is then played out. Thereafter, practical circumstances may, almost immediately, call the spellbound spectator or wonder-struck victim, back to practical reality. With that recall, the psycho-neurosis (aka emotional constipation) is instantly set up.

We can now reach almost the same understanding Delboeuf and Binet arrived at as early as 1891, when they wrote: *"We can now explain how the hypnotist promotes cure. He puts the subject back into the state in which his trouble first appeared, and uses words to combat that trouble, as it makes a fresh emergence"*.
Breuer and Freud took that understanding a step further, because it is not the hypnotist, but the patient or client, who must use words in order to combat his own trouble.

The victim of a psycho-neurosis has to be taken into hypnosis, or go into self-hypnosis (a reverie or daydream) and then – recall the event – feel the emotion, and let it flow by shouting or sobbing, or discharge it by talking about it. If the recall takes place during hypnosis in a consulting room, there is no problem. The client can speak, scream or sob. That is the purpose of a consulting room. If the recall takes place during a daydream there may be a problem. Let us hope that the daydream, in which the trauma surfaces, happens in some place, where we can let go. Bedrooms and toilets are just as good for that purpose as the hypno-analyst's consulting room.

Bus stops, however, are different. Bus services being what they are, the wait for a bus frequently induces day dreams, but bus stops are not very good places for the purpose of catharsis. Nevertheless, the discharge of emotional constipation is such a blessing, that it is well worth a moment of embarrassment in front of one or two disinterested spectators.

The worst place to recall a traumatic experience is in front of the television cameras. Unfortunately, that often happens, when accident victims or war veterans recount their experiences in front of an audience of millions. Then the audience sees a veteran on the brink of tears, and thus on the verge of catharsis from some awful trauma. The tragedy is that the veteran usually feels compelled by his social training to choke back the repressed emotion, which has blighted his life for decades. It would be best for the old soldier's health and for the audience's better understanding of psycho-neuroses, if he sobbed - heroically. Pride should never stand in the way of catharsis.

Children can not be expected to recognise such moments for catharsis in every day life, but such moments can be provided for them. When disturbed children are relaxed, they can be asked whether they can think of some time when they were very sad, or ashamed or felt naughty (i.e. guilty) or felt bullied. They can be told, that if they remember anything like that, they can "Blow it Away" The action of blowing in relation to any one of those emotions which rings a bell, is enough overt physical response to the old experience to discharge any related emotional constipation.

There is no reason to ask the children, whether they did remember such incidents. It will be evident from the way they blow, whether they remembered something that had troubled them. There is no reason why adults should not use that method on themselves in the privacy of their bedrooms, or even at a bus stop. Just remember, one blow may not be enough. Keep blowing until you are fed up with it. Catharsis might as well be done properly.

A perceived traumatic threat can be met by
FIGHT - FLIGHT or FRIGHT
Fight and Flight are done in the waking state.
Fright takes you into a hypnoid state
Editor

Chapter 30 - IMMUNE SYSTEM

It is the function of the body's immune system to identify invaders, and to destroy them. That is an organic function, but like almost everything else, it can be affected by the mind.

It is a well known fact that people, who suddenly have a lot of troubles, are prone to get one organic illness or another, to add to their woes. Under the influence of stress the immune system loses its potency. In consequence those alien entities like bacteria or viruses survive, and multiply. The patient then gets an organic illness for psycho-neurotic reasons.

The totality of stress, which undermines the immune system, may in part be due to present troubles, and in part to the constant presence of an old psycho-neurosis. Although psychic problems can create the situation in which an organic illness can take hold, that organic illness can not be cured by psycho-therapy. The organic illness has to run its course, but restoration of the immune system, by removal of the psycho-neurotic stress, would facilitate the natural cure.

The same effect can be observed in the case of organic injuries, whether accidental or due to an operation. Every injury invokes the functions of the immune system, and wounds heal more quickly, if the healing process is not obstructed by alien agencies. That should not be confused with cases, where the rogue electronic impulses from a psycho-neurosis inhibit the healing process itself, as it primary affect.

The effects of psycho-neuroses on the immune system are bad enough. They can be summarised by saying, that if the immune system is damaged, it can not do its job properly. That is easy to understand. Equally, one can not blame a healthy immune system, if it attacks transplanted organs, because their chromosomes are strange, and they seem to be alien bodies.

If the immune system can attack the alien cells arriving from an organ transplant, why does it not always deal with cancer cells, which are another sort of alien bodies? Could it be that the immune system has been undermined by the totality of the cancer patient's stress? Patients sometimes recover spontaneously from cancer. They inexplicably get remission. Is that when the immune system has reasserted itself, because the totality of stress had been reduced for one reason or another ?

Less comprehensible than the failure of the immune system is the auto-immune EFFECT. Perhaps the phenomenon, which occurs when damage to the immune system by a psycho-neurosis, causes the system to destroy healthy cells (which it should be protecting) is really an auto-immune AFFECT. Could it be, that the auto-immune effects (phenomena) are really auto-immune affects, the causes of which are psycho-neuroses ?

Auto-immune problems are too numerous to name. One example of such attacks on the healthy parts of a body is the baldness, which develops when the immune system attacks hair follicles. Unlike organic loss of hair, the loss of hair due to a psycho-neurosis is reversible. If the psycho-neurosis is resolved, hair growth is restored.

There are many causes for infertility, some of which are undoubtedly psycho-neurotic. It may be that infertility too, is sometimes due to an auto-immune affect. I will say that again: It may be that infertility is sometimes the effect of an auto-immune affect, which causes the immune system to attack healthy cells.

If an overactive immune system can attack hair follicles, which are genetically identical to the rest of the body, how much more could a defective immune system attack the gametes of either sex, which have only half the body's approved chromosomes, and are to that extent alien. The chromosomes of the embryo, half of which are certainly alien, might also be attacked by an immune system thrown out of kilter by the stress of one or more psychoneuroses.

Such a so-called auto-immune "effect" is only one of the ways in which a psycho-neurosis may prevent conception. Another is by way of throwing the whole delicate hormone system out of kilter. It may be that more psychical research needs to be done into the psychic causes of both infertility and cancer. (See Chapter 43)

Troubles rarely come singly.
Proverb

Chapter 31 - SMOKING

Smoking may be the direct affect, which a psycho-neurosis has chosen as the outlet for its loose innervation. Where the smoking is due to a psycho-neurosis, it also provides an example of the diversionary tactics, which are a part of resistance.

When we are actively engaged in a task, we are firmly in the normal waking state. When the task is completed, or when we take a break, we may relax, and could slide into a daydream or a reverie. For psych-neurotics, that opens up the possibility of bumping into the trauma and the associated emotions, which lurk in their subconscious mind. At that point a diversionary tactic becomes a useful adjunct to successful resistance.

People with that problem could reach for a sweet, and be distracted by fiddling with the wrapping paper, or they could reach for a packet of cigarettes. The latter is a better diversion, because they have to:-

> Take out the packet of cigarettes,
> open the packet,
> select a cigarette,
> calculate when they will need the next packet,
> extract a cigarette,
> put the cigarette into the mouth,
> close the packet,
> put the packet away,
> reach for the matches or lighter,
> and strike a light.

Now things get even better. They have to guard a living flame.

> That calls for undivided attention,
> while setting the cigarette alight,
> coughing for ten minutes,
> guarding the living fire,
> disposing of the ashes,
> and stubbing out the cigarette, not to mention the ashtray.

During all that time, the incipient danger from the repressed trauma has been obviated. The surfacing of the memory of the traumatic incident has been avoided What a relief. Paradoxically, the smokers can relax, despite the fact that nicotine is a stimulant. If they are lucky, the trauma will not make another immediate attempt to resurface.

The same principle applies to a greater or lesser extent to any other diversionary tactic. It could be nail biting. The nails are always handy. The task of biting another bit off already badly bitten nails requires close attention. In that way the conscious mind is fully occupied, and the momentary danger of re-emergence of the old trauma is temporarily again averted.

Chapter 32 - SUICIDE

The aim of this chapter is to consider the unanswered questions about those, who commit suicide without an overt, clearly identifiable reason. If a suicide has anything to do with psycho-neurosis, there is a problem. On the one hand we can not ask the people who committed suicide what went on in their mind to make them commit suicide. On the other hand, there is no point in asking live psycho-neurotics about their problems, because they do not know what they are. If you have read this book, you will be aware that, if the potential suicides knew the exact cause of their problems, and reacted accordingly, their problems would have disappeared.

Since neither of those two sources of inside knowledge is available to us, we must try to examine the subject from first principles. There may have been one massive trauma, or many smaller ones (or indeed both). In any event the suicides will have struggled against the emergence of those traumas day and night, waking and sleeping, merely to do nothing more than stay on an even keel. They would have had to negotiate their way around the blocked areas in the mind in order to perform any function, or to take any decision. They would have been essentially inefficient and (in their own eyes) unsuccessful. They would not have had much pleasure in anything. The windmills of their mind would have gone round and round without respite, and when they tried to sleep, the traumas would have turned into nightmares that woke them up. Alternatively, they may have had black depression.

Every break they tried to take from their other preoccupations, would only have served to leave the field free for the traumas to rise up from the subconscious. Then they would have to be wrestled down again, and that struggle would go on and on. There would be no light at the end of that tunnel, and they can not see any way out. Nobody has ever told them that, if a door will not open outwards, try opening it inwards. Such people are usually conspicuous for great will power, and continue to fight with themselves, but in the end even they give up hope. The only way out of the hell in the mind seems to be to throw the final switch, and commit suicide.

The worst of it is that in retrospect, those traumas are rarely worth a single sleepless night (let alone suicide). Once they have been brought out of the subconscious memories of yesteryear into the clear light of today, those traumas disappear. The potential suicides, the windmills of whose mind keep going restlessly round and round, need to be told that there is a way out. It is called catharsis (See Chapter 4) and it leads to surprising, liberating enlightenment. Everything about the past suddenly becomes clear, and life becomes enjoyable.

One thing is certain. A prospective suicide needs help. Such help can be sought from anybody or everybody, but that "everybody" should undoubtedly include an hypno-analyst. It is a virtual certainty, that after a course of hypno-analysis the prospective suicide's perspective on life will be quite different, because some (if not necessarily all) the troublesome psychoneuroses, which contribute to the totality of stress (in this case, distress) will have been removed. The colloquial daemons, which drive some individuals to suicide, are merely psycho-neuroses.

Assisted suicides need separate consideration. They pose special problems, because the sanctioning official and the suicide's assistant have to make a judgment about the would-be suicide's state of mind. They have to decide, whether the person applying for assisted suicide is of "sound mind".

Once more we are up against the problem of appropriate vocabulary, because the term "sound mind" needs to be defined. If we disqualify unsound minds, we are left with two sorts of "sound minds". One sort of sound mind is the kind that functions perfectly without any blocks or hang-ups. The other sort of sound mind may be brilliant, but has some of its functions distorted by emotional constipation (alias psycho-neurosis). That fact may not be obvious, but it may be very relevant, and in that respect the super-logical are the most suspect. At the very least, the affect of the suicides' emotional constipation may cause a distorted view of the position they are in. At worst the affect of their emotional constipation may be self-punishment in the form of suicide. Such suicides would no more know why they have this death wish, than a girl who slashes her upper arms knows why she is doing it.

There are therefore two sorts of "sound mind". One sort is a mind that is free of any kind of psycho-neurosis. The other has one or more irrational blocks. The only way to test, whether the applicant for assisted suicide is free of any psycho-neurosis which could bend their mind to such an extreme solution, is by asking them to agree to hypno-analysis. Compared to suicide, hypno-analysis in pursuit of the Greek injunction to "Know Thyself" is not an ordeal. It is a small price to pay for the assistant's license. Refusal to go through that door to the apparently desired objective, could be seen as the very resistance, which is such an important feature of psycho-neuroses. It follows that assisted suicides provide that special opportunity to see into the minds of the would be suicides, which is not available in cases of unassisted suicides. If, after hypno-analysis the applicant is still bent on assisted suicide, the application could be considered on its merits. Conversely it might transpire, that in the face of surprising liberating enlightenment, the applicant has a totally changed view of the world, and of his or her place in it.

Hypno-analysis of applicants for assisted suicide would also provide a clearer picture of what help is needed by the people who might commit suicide unilaterally.

Chapter 33 - RELIGION

Whereas religion plays no part in analytical hypno-therapy, it may happen to play a part in the aetiology of a psycho-neurosis. Accordingly, religion may be involved in resolving it. The cure by Jesus of the lame beggar at the Pool of Bethesda is recorded in Chapter 5 of St.John's gospel. The beggar's guilt was resolved by having his sins forgiven by somebody known as a holy man. That miracle is probably the best know example of the discharge of a psycho-neurosis.

The most likely emotional ingredients of a psycho-neurosis are fear, shame or guilt. The nature of an individual's belief system can therefore provide scope for guilt at transgressing the commandments of his or her religion, or shame at having transgressed them. Thus religious expiation during a visit to a shrine, or under other religious circumstances, can potentially resolve a psycho-neurosis, by discharging the emotional constipation. In religious terms that is a miracle. In terms of psycho-therapy that is catharsis.

One man may feel guilt at having transgressed the commandment: "Thou shalt not kill." Conversely a man, who has a religious duty to avenge the death of a relative, might feel shame at having missed a golden opportunity to murder his brother's killer. There is no need for us to speculate about the scope, which one religion or another provides for psycho-neuroses. The possible variations on that theme are infinite and imponderable. Suffice it to quote the case of a South Sea islander, who died after inadvertently breaking a taboo.

It seems that on one of the South Sea islands the chiefs had a different diet to ordinary islanders. The warriors took their food with them on the warpath, and chiefs had the duty to bury uneaten food, so that it could not fall into the hands of ordinary islanders. Unfortunately, a careless chief failed to bury his surplus ration. Another warrior found the chief's food, and ate it. When that islander discovered that he had broken the taboo, he figuratively "turned his face to the wall", and died. Since psycho-neuroses can be fatal, it may be, that it is just such cases which give rise to the saying: "Only the good die young".

Another example involving religion is provided by one of Freud's cases which involved a young Jewish woman and a saying colloquial at the time. People used to warn against using another person's comb, in order not to contract lice, and so jokingly it was said: "in order not to mix the breed". In those days it was still taboo for Jews to marry out of the Jewish community, but the young woman was involved with a Christian. In analysis, the association of ideas from comb to "mixing of the breeds" revealed where her problem lay.

On the basis of an understanding of psychoneuroses it is easy to see, that the Roman Catholic confessional could have a direct beneficial effect, by releasing the penitent of a religious psycho-neurosis. The mind being what it is, even a psycho-neurosis with a tenuous connection to religion might be resolved in the confession box. Therefore the confessional could be of even greater benefit to members of that persuasion, if priest were better versed in the subject of psycho-neurosis and catharsis.

In that connection it is worth noting that the "Seven Deadly Sins", namely anger, envy, greed, lust, gluttony, sloth and pride are all emotions, but you can not tell people not to have emotions. They come of their own accord. If you have got them, you have got them. All you can tell people to do about them is to find them, acknowledge them, and discharge them. What you must not do is, harbour them.

Pride is said to be the worst of the seven deadly sins. Pride is indeed the worst, because it is pride, which prevents individuals from accepting experiences which conflict with their own view of themselves – their egos. The shock of that conflict then leads to a psycho-neuroses, which can indeed be fatal. The humbleness of kneeling on the floor, and bowing the head to the ground is a good antidote to pride. It may open the door to catharsis, if pride was the cause of emotional constipation. Every religion is to some extent intellectual but, where it lays claim to a healing function, it is in contact with the subconscious part of the psyche at some point.

One more thing should be said in this chapter. The subject of religious self-punishment is too important to be casually listed in the chapter on the diversity of affects. It is, of course, openly acknowledge under the name of penance. Such penitence can take many forms, of which self-incarceration in a monastery or cloister is just one example. Whatever form the penitential self-punishment takes, people often give their lives to it. What needs to be said about it in the context of this book, is that the people who inflict such punishment on themselves, almost certainly rationalise their behaviour. They attribute their self-punishment to a different sin to the one which caused their psycho-neurosis, because they can not remember the latter. Like everyone else, they need to recall the real cause of their religious psycho-neurosis, and discharge the relevant emotion.

While the hypnoid state of religious meditation provides a suitable opportunity for recalling the relevant trauma, it does not usually take place in the best venue for the overt physical expression needed for catharsis. On the other hand the confessional provides an excellent opportunity for overt physical expression (at least in the form of words or tears), but it does not usually provide an opportunity for the necessary hypnoid state The problem is to provide an environment in which both ingredients for catharsis are present.

✶✶✶✶✶✶✶✶

"Pride comes before the fall"
Proverb

Chapter 34 – DIVORCE

There does not seem to be any specific hypno-analytical expertise or anecdotal evidence on the subject of divorce, but I am prepared to venture the opinion, that in a high proportion of cases the reasons for a divorce are fundamentally psycho-neurotic. Many participants in that kind of social misadventure would gladly echo the sentiment of the peasant at a crossroad in County Mayo. When asked the way to Dublin, he said: "If I were going to Dublin, I would not start from here". Unfortunately for those on the brink of a divorce, here is where they are. Faced with that misfortune, people need to get a new perspective on their relationship. A new perspective would undoubtedly come, if they were not seeing each other through the fog of their respective psychoneuroses. Therefore it would be as well to consider the effect of psycho-neuroses on divorcees themselves, and on society in general.

If a married couple have no other ties, they may well amicably choose to go their separate ways, and take their individual psychoneuroses with them. The more likely scenario is that the decision to divorce is unilateral. In that case the offending partner seeking a divorce may have found the behavior, mannerisms, unreasonable demands, recurrent indispositions or other irritations from their partner intolerable. The aggrieved partner might reasonably say that the "offending" spouse needs to have his or her "head examined". That assessment may well be correct. Those shortcomings may all be psycho-neurotic, and it is all the other partners "fault". On that basis, the partner with the evident psycho-neurotic quirks, is the one who ought seek help from an hypno-analyst.

On the other hand, the "offending" partner is not the one contemplating or initiating the divorce. The partner who is contemplating a divorce or separation may have psycho-neuroses of his or her own, which are not as evident as those of the "offending" partner. They may, however, be just as relevant. The partner contemplating the divorce should therefore be the first to take whatever steps are necessary to resolve his or her own psycho-neuroses. Once the preconceptions, aims and attitudes based on those psycho-neuroses have gone, the "offending" partner's shortcomings may be seen in a different light. Thereafter it may, or may not, be necessary to invite the ostensibly "offending" partner to clear the backlog of his or her emotional constipation.

That is not to say, that an offending partner who is well aware of his or her own shortcomings, but "can't help it", should not take whatever unilateral steps are necessary to get the problem resolved, with or without the help of a hypno-analyst. It is always the will to resolve your own neurosis that counts, even when helped by an analyst.

Where there are children, all the above considerations apply, but other factors also come into play. The stability of the family is at stake, and traumatic situations, which could cause psycho-neuroses in the couple's children ought to be avoided. Even if a divorce has to proceed, a couple without psycho-neuroses is more likely to achieve an amicable separation. Such a couple is also more likely to maintain an amicable relationship after the divorce. That would certainly be of benefit to the couple's children.

Last but by no means least it should be said, that people who have shed the blocks and hang-ups they have dragged around with them for years, will almost certainly be better parents than they were, or would have been, while they still had those blocks and hang-ups.

****

Psycho-analysis is Hypno-analysis done without hypnosis.
In consequence it may take months, if not years
Editor

****

Chapter 35 - SLEEPLESSNESS

Sleeplessness is no different to any other psycho-neurosis. They are all due to a greater or lesser emotional upheaval, and subsequent emotional constipation. Chronic sleeplessness may be due to the dreams or nightmares by which a psycho-neurosis can manifest itself during sleep. What distinguishes sleeplessness from other psycho-neurotic affects, is that it provides a special opportunity for do-it-yourself psycho-therapy.

Most repressed and suppressed experiences have a tendency to surface temporarily during quiet periods. They may do so even on a busy day, but then the pressure of events facilitate their re-submergence into the subconscious. Unfortunately, such a momentary opportunity for catharsis is quickly gone. For people with chronic sleeplessness things are different. For them there are three possible scenarios. In the most extreme cases the sufferer avoids going to bed, or having spent a few hours wrestling with their hidden tormentor, they get up again, and find something to occupy their conscious mind.

In less extreme cases, in between short snatches of shallow sleep the sufferers toss and turn in bed all night long. They get up in the morning, more tired than they were when they went to bed. The constant struggle to keep the unwelcome memory of their traumatic experience at bay, wears them out. They welcome the relief from their struggle provided by the activities of the day, which they find more restful than their attempts to sleep.

The third scenario is to some extent the worst. In the silent watches of the night the sufferer may drift into a hypnoid state, and recall the traumatic experience which is the cause of their sleeplessness. They review and relive it, over and over again, but fail to react to that experience. In consequence the trauma remains undisturbed in the hypnoid state, into which it was encapsulated. When the sufferers return to the waking state, and gets out of bed in the morning, they are not consciously aware that the relevant trauma exists.

The tragedy of this third scenario is that this special opportunity for catharsis is potentially available for eight hours in every twenty-four, but it is often passed up. The sleepless victims of such psycho-neuroses are lying in bed anyway. They might just as well put the time to good use, by taking measures to rid themselves of that encumbrance. Instead of tossing and turning, they need to take active steps to relax. That may take some practice, but it is worth the effort. They undoubtedly have the time to practice. It is better than spending the night just tossing and turning in bed.

The problem for the sufferer from sleeplessness is how to relax. There are, of course, many ways of relaxing, some more apparent than real, but the simplest way is to start with three or four deep breaths. Then all the separate muscles of the body should be relaxed in turn, from the top of the head to the tips of the fingers, and then again to the tips of the toes. If at first you don't succeed, try, try and try again. You have got plenty of time. We are talking about sleeplessness.

The time in bed should not be allowed to go to waste. The sufferers from sleeplessness have got nothing to lose, except their sleeplessness.

Once relaxed, the insomniacs will very likely fall asleep. In that case, one of their objectives has been achieved anyway. Alternatively the insomniacs may drift into self-hypnosis, also known as genuine meditation. Then the memories will come drifting by in an illogical sequence, but in an endless chain of unseen associations.

Finally confronted by such a traumatic memory, the insomniacs will probably fail to realise that their feelings were involved. That is where the term emotional constipation, as an alternative to psycho-neurosis, is at its most apt. Instead of being discharged, the relevant emotion had got stuck, and it remains stuck. Unless the emotional content of the remembered experience is identified, its disturbing affect remains undiminished.

In re-viewing the experience the sufferer has to say to himself or herself: "Yes, I know that experience only too well, but how did I feel about it ? What did I feel about it ? What should I have felt about it ?" The answers to those questions have to be said out loud, and once identified, repeated as often as possible. In those happy circumstances, no attempt should be made to regain "control". It was control that caused the trouble in the first place. In the optimum circumstances the answer, which the subconscious mind brings up, will be validated by the appropriate emotional discharge like anger or tears. If such spontaneous emotional discharge does not take place, catharsis can be achieved by speaking to the ceiling - out loud. As likely as not, the relevant discharge will be followed by a yawn.

Whatever the memory was, say it out loud. That may be embarrassing, even in bed, but it is well worth while. It is not a sign that it is time to call in the men in white coats. On the contrary, it is a sign that a trauma has been addressed, and a psycho-neurosis is being resolved.

****

If you would like to change one moment in your life, what is it ?
Feel that moment - and say it out loud
Editor

****

Chapter 36 - TELEVISION

There seems to be a general perception that the younger generation is more peculiar than previous generations, and that the problem is getting worse. It is, of course, difficult to compare one generation with another. Nevertheless, it would be surprising if that perception were not correct. Through the media of films and television children have so much more scope for real and imaginary experiences than were available to their forebears. Some of those newly available experiences may be traumatic to a susceptible child. That has lead some people to ascribe the troubles of the present generation to the sex and violence purveyed by those media.

It is an attractive theory, but it is facile. Although it is true to say that the modern media put ideas into people's minds, which they would otherwise not have had, that of itself does not give anybody a trauma. All that sex and violence usually just washes over people, or at worst is "in one ear and out the other". If it is absorbed, it usually only amounts to useless information.

The real cause of the problem is that the programs, even when full of sex and violence, are often so boring that children slumped in front of the television set lapse into a hypnoid state. What they see, and what they fantasise from the program, provides them with experiences, for which their minds are not prepared. Those experiences may be virtual, but if the child is stimulated, the experience can seem very real. When the children come out of their reverie or daydream, they have no notion of how their experience has affected them.

That is best illustrated by the case of a lad, who claimed in analysis that he had been a soldier of the Wehrmacht in a previous incarnation. He appeared to be able to describe every detail of his service. The truth, however, was that he had been sitting in front of a television set, watching a film about the first world war. The story was about a German soldier, who went on leave behind the lines during a lull in the fighting. There, he met up with a local girl, and they were shown having sex.

The lad had been watching the film with one eye, while perusing a girly magazine with the other. That brought on an orgasm. At the precise moment when he ejaculated, his mother had come in at the front door, and he was jerked out of his hypnoid state.

If he had not been in a hypnoid state while watching television, the shock of being caught with semen in one hand, and the girly magazine in the other, was certainly enough to put him into a hypnoid state. The subsequent forced escape from the hypnoid state to deal with the immediate reality of his mother's return, blotted the incident from his conscious mind.

Incidents affecting other children, who go into a hypnoid mode while watching television, will probably not be quite so colourful, but they account for many of the health problems, learning difficulties and behavioural aberrations, which mar their lives during their school days and beyond. There can be no doubt, that the introduction of high definition and three dimensional television will serve to heighten the effect of the virtual experiences on the viewer, and hence increase the likelihood of a psychic affect, especially in the case of children.

It should not be supposed that the causative experience is necessarily of sex or violence. The virtual experience could just as well be a story of loving motherhood, if the child thinks that it is not the recipient of similar treatment, and infers that its mother does not love it. What a child may phantasise in the face of an intense experience is unpredictable and unfathomable. It will probably also be harmless, but if it leads to an emotion, which can not be effectively processed at the time (probably guilt in the case of the boy who thought he was a German soldier in a previous incarnation) it will produce a puzzling psycho-neurosis.

Subsequently, the affect of a psycho-neuroses thus acquired, will have an effect on the children's development and on their careers. Those affects stay with them throughout their lives, unless one of three things happens to discharge them. They may chance to wear away in the process of growing up, they may be discharged by a later relevant event (life experience) or they can be purged by catharsis, achieved via meditation, or via induced hypnosis. Prevention, however, is always better than cure. When television is not actively being watched, it should be switched off.

Children can, of course, be "stage struck" by drama seen on television, as well as by drama seen on the boards. Conversely, drama on stage or on television can amount to a "life experience" leading to the discharge of emotional constipation, or the release of a hang-up.

Many emotive subjects are extensively covered on television. Psycho-neurosis is not one of them. As part of its educational function, television has a duty to spread a better understanding of the ins and outs of the hypnoid state.

Any person, who does not act rationally, has a hidden agenda.
That hidden agenda is probably a psycho-neurosis
Editor

✳✳✳✳✳✳✳✳✳

Chapter 37 - DELAYED AFFECT

The majority of psycho-neuroses have their origin in early childhood, because that is when emotions are at their fiercest. In childhood, the discharge of those emotions caused by some real or imagined trauma, is usually visible in the form of tears or temper tantrums. If that emotional discharge does not take place, the substitute affect from such traumas is not necessarily visible at the time. That makes the later appearance of the substitute affect all the more bewildering.

In the time between the relevant trauma, and its subsequent manifestation many years later, the child may have some unidentifiable blocks or hang-ups, which are caused by the repression. In that case the child's learning ability and decision taking will have been affected, but there may be no identifiable affect. The outward relevant affect does not become noticeable, until a disaster stresses the nervous system later in life. At that point, some very noticeable affect like depression, can set in.

Such a depression, or other affect, can not be resolved by identification of the current trauma. Only identification and discharge of the trauma, apparently dormant from early childhood, can lift the depression. Volumes of advices have been written about methods of dealing with depression, and its apparent cause. Those methods are at best palliative. The cause of the depression is the childhood trauma, and the later catastrophe is only the trigger. The fact that the source of a current disability may have to be sought in early childhood, should be of as much interest to insurance companies, as it would be to the disabled victim of an accident.

After the evident injuries to an accident victim have healed, some pain or disability, which did not exist before the accident, may remain. It is then easy to assume that the disability or pain is a somatic problem, which owes it origin to the injuries suffered in the accident. That assumption may, of course, be correct. The victim of the accident may in fact be left with a physical disability or life long pain.

On the other hand, that assumption is not necessarily correct. The Latin tag *post hoc ergo propter hoc,* meaning: *"after that, therefore because of that"*, is intended as a warning against making such assumptions. In fact the post accident pain or disability may not necessarily be physical, but could be psycho-somatic. They may in fact owe their origin to a childhood trauma, which has lain, so to speak dormant, for many years. (See Chapters 13 & 17) If that has happened, no amount of after care will cure that kind of post accident affect.

What is assumed to be a post accident effect on the body, may in fact be the post accident affect of a childhood trauma. By making the erroneous *post hoc ergo propter hoc* assumption, the accident victim will accept his fate as part of the accident, and the insurance company will pay up.

The only means by which the doubt about the nature of those affects can be resolved is by what Freud called "Breuer's method", but two obstacles have to be overcome, before an insurance company can effectively invoke it.

The first obstacle is that the insured victim would have to give consent to such an investigation. Fortunately, the greater the disability involved, the more likely the accident victim is to give his or her conscious consent to hypno-analysis. Consciously the accident victim would probably like to be rid of the troublesome disabilities.

The other obstacle to successful resolution of such disabilities is that hypno-analysis may be blocked by the secondary benefits arising from the psycho-neurosis. (See Chapter 39) If the client would receive almost as much from the insurance claim, as he could potentially earn by continued use of his or her pre-accident skills, analysis is likely to be subconsciously blocked. Even if the claimant is a capped international, and would apparently like to be selected in the future, the reality of the secondary benefit may hinder or prevent resolution of the psycho-somatic after affect of the childhood trauma.

****

Emotional constipation makes you a different person to the one you would be, if you did not have emotional constipation.

Editor

****

Chapter 38 - SELF- PUNISHMENT

One of the forms of affect which a psycho-neurosis can create, is self-punishment. An apparently obvious example of that malpractice is flagellation. That form of religious chastisement may merely be conformity in a group of people, some of who do really feel the need for such self-punishment. Alternatively, it may be practised by their people in order to score brownie points in a religious group. Not even the participants can tell, whether they are making a logical decision, or whether they were motivated (if that is the right word) by a psycho-neurosis to participate in that activity.

Whereas flagellation is usually done by men in public, self-slashing is more often done by girls in private. The girls then go to great lengths to hide their wounds and scars. It is a form of self-mutilation. Every form of self mutilation is probably a self- punishment, except that the perpetrators do not know why they are doing it. Even a suicide, who may know that the constant struggle in his mind has made life unbearable, did not know the reason why his mind had made life unbearable.

Nail biting, and indeed excessive nail cutting is a form of self-mutilation. The same is true of hair pulling. Sometimes there are reasons for pulling out a hair or two, but even that ostensible reason may be suspect, because the hair puller or eyebrow plucker may have a view of him or herself, which is distorted by a psycho-neurosis.

Ear rings are a fashion accessory, which may be justified on the grounds that they are customary. An African beauty, whose earlobes are pulled down as far as the shoulder, may be entirely free of any sort of neurosis. She does it, because it is a social custom, but the decision to have an adult woman's ears pierced may be no different to the decision to have studs put into the lips, or nipples, or even into the tongue. Such studs are almost certainly a form of self- mutilation, with its origins in a psycho-neurosis.

The same is true of anything, which the perpetrators know to be bad for their health. The smokers who say: "I know that smoking will kill me" and the alcoholics who knows that alcohol is destroying their liver, but keep smoking or drinking anyway, would not be doing it, if it were not for their psycho-neuroses. That fact does, of course, apply to other substance abuse, even if it is (only) glue sniffing.

Unfortunately, self-punishment is not confined to mechanical or chemical damage. Mental torture, if only in the form of persistent disappointment, is another one of the infinite number of ways in which a person can punish an imagined, but repressed misdeed or misadventure.

Gambling is a particularly useful (if that is the right word) form of self-punishment. The longer the odds are, the more certain is the punishment. The occasional win only serves to enable the penitent to continue that form of self-torture. Any means of denying oneself a source of enjoyment, on whatever pretext, is a form of self-punishment. That is seen at its most spectacular, when an exceptionally talented player regularly gets to semi-finals or even finals, but unaccountably, never wins the championship.

How can one establish, whether a "losing streak" at gambling, or a losing streak in the finals of championships is really just bad luck, or is in fact self-punishment due to a psycho-neurosis ? You've guessed it. There is only one way to tell, and that is by looking for a potential cause in the subconscious mind.

It is very unlikely that a logical connection will be found between the damaging behaviour and the original cause of the psycho-neurosis. One thing is certain. Whatever childhood trauma is found and discharged, the individual will become a more effective person, even if the resolved trauma did not relate directly to lost bets, lost matches or lost opportunities.

"Inexplicable accidents are another example of that genre of misadventures. The point is, that there is no difference between inexplicable accidents causing damage, and "unknown viruses causing illness. Directly, or indirectly, they are probably both the affect of psycho-neuroses.

"If it's worth saying, it's worth saying twice".
Proverb

Chapter 39 - SECONDARY BENEFITS

Benefits are where you find them. We already met some of them in Chapter 37. The benefit of catharsis, however achieved, is that the affect manifested by the psycho-neurosis comes to an abrupt end. The psycho-somatic affliction, the phobia, the behavioural quirk is gone, and the efficient working of the liberated mind is restored. All those can be said to be real benefits.

The benefits from getting a psycho-neurosis in the first place are more illusory. They fall into two categories. The primary benefit of getting the trauma tucked away into the hypnoid state is the avoidance of the rush of emotion, which the victim would have had to face while in the waking state. That is what psycho-neuroses are about, and in theory, they should be resolved as soon as possible.

The secondary benefit of the consequent, persistent psycho-neurosis, is certainly variable. It depends on the lifestyle of the neurotic. The secondary benefit may be an incapacity allowance. It may be that the victim does not have to get up in the morning and go to work, or that he gets the type of work he prefers, or that he gets care and attention he would not otherwise get. It may be that it is so much nicer in a warm hospital bed, among other patients, than home alone in a cold flat. Those are all secondary benefits

The secondary benefit may be something one could not possibly guess at, or of which the patient himself may be only dimly aware. It may, on the other hand, be blindingly obvious. That is why Christ asked the lame beggar at the Pool of Bethesda, whether he wanted to be healed. Far from being a silly question, it was perceptive. At the sacred pool the beggar had a livelihood as a beggar. What would he live on, if he were cured ? In the event the beggar roundly renounced his secondary benefit. He wanted to be cured without reservations, and his belief in the annulment of his guilt by the holy man discharged his psychic paralysis, and enabled him to "take up his bed and walk".

Not everyone with a psychoneurosis is quite so willing to give up the secondary benefit. That is why many of those, who appear to be suffering from the affects of a psycho-neurosis, and complain about it persistently, suddenly lose interest when the possibility of a cure appears on the horizon. They have come to terms with their affliction, and a new world without it seems much too daunting.

Such an attitude may seem perverse, but secondary benefits are real. What they are depends upon the individual's attitude to life. That is well illustrated by the case of a married woman with more than one symptom, who came for therapy in a wheel chair, and had the effect of the therapy explained to her. As soon as she understood, that she was in danger of being freed of all her symptoms, instead of only the ones she wished to shed, she declined the therapy.

She explained her decision by saying that she had her present life style effectively organised. Her husband did the shopping, her son did the cooking and her daughter did the cleaning. She did not really need to be able to get out of her wheel chair.

The primary benefit of avoiding the emotion associated with her trauma (whatever that may have been) plus the secondary benefit of having her family organised around her, were enough. The loss of those two benefits would have been too great a price to pay for the "mere" surprising, liberating enlightenment which catharsis would have brought. Secondary benefits are very real (See Chapter 30) but they are not healthy, and they leave the "beneficiary" with the unseen effect of the inefficient working of the mind. (See Chapter 19)

"Psycho-analysis is spending $40 an hour to squeal on your mother"

Mike Connolly.

Chapter 40 - THE SURGERY OPTION

There have been psycho-neuroses with a somatic affect since the dawn of time. The Ancient Greeks knew of them. People have gone to priests with them, and their confessions will at times have had a curative effect. People have also consulted doctors about them ever since antiquity, but usually to no avail. It is therefore important to acknowledge, that it was two medical practitioners, who recognised the difference between psycho-neuroses and somatic neuroses, thereby opening the door to psycho-therapy.

It is then important to appreciate the relationship of this relatively new form of therapy to orthodox medicine. Psycho-therapy can be complementary to orthodox medical care, as by non-pharmacological analgesia, or to speed the healing of wounds. Conversely, orthodox medicine can be complementary to psycho-therapy, if the application of a soothing cream relieves the itch caused by an allergy, while the patient embarks on hypno-analysis to find the cause of the allergy.

On the other hand, orthodox medicine can never be an alternative to hypno-analysis. Where a psycho-neurosis is involved, psycho-therapy is the only therapy. The malfunction of a limb can be attacked by surgery, but that would only deal with the symptom. It would not discharge the psycho-neurosis, which may find another outlet for its aberrant innervation.

If you have read the preceding pages of this book, you will appreciate that neither complementary therapy nor alternative therapy is effective in resolving a psycho-somatic affliction. If there is a psycho-somatic illness, neither medication nor the knife can have any curative effect. In cases, which are caused by the suppression of the emotion attached to a traumatic experience, psycho-therapy is the only effective treatment.

Two more points need to be considered. The minor one, already mentioned, is that complementary treatments, like a skin cream or sedative medication, could make life easier for the patient while working through psycho-therapy. The major comment can not be too strongly emphasised. In any situation, in which both surgery and psycho-therapy could be contemplated as the apparently available as explorable options, psycho-therapy should precede surgery.

Psycho-therapy, in its analytic form, can do no harm. At worst it fails to discover any association with the symptoms under consideration. If collateral traumatic experiences are discharged, the patient will be able to withstand the traumas of surgery better than if the psychic traumas were still praying on his mind. The optimum scenario would be that the symptoms, for which surgery is contemplated, are found to have had a psychosomatic cause, and disappear. In such a happy case surgery will prove to be unnecessary.

Conversely, surgery is itself traumatic, at least in the organic sense. It may fail to achieve its objective, but it may have unintended consequences. Some damage done by the surgery can not be undone. It would be as distressing for the surgeon as it would be for the patient, if the surgery failed in its objective, and subsequent psycho-therapy resolved the problem.

It is not a question of whether psycho-therapy is better than surgery. It might well be that surgery succeeds in its objective of abating a certain pain, or by stopping some involuntary muscular activity, but the psychoneurosis would remain. That would leave the patient with the other affects of the psycho-neurosis, and the very real danger that the still available innervation would find another outlet, thereby producing a new symptom.

It can safely be said, that if psycho-therapy fails to solve the immediate problem, and surgery does ultimately prove essential, the psycho-therapy has not been wasted. Very few people go through life without some major or minor hang-up. After psycho-therapy by means of hypno-analysis, the patients would face the operation with a more balanced mind. They would be much better able to cope with the surgery itself, with the physical trauma of the surgery, and with the healing process after surgery.

For all those reasons psycho-therapy and surgery should be very carefully considered in relation to each other. Whereas people tend to turn to orthodox medicine, and regard psycho-therapy as a last resort, hypno-analysis should be the penultimate option in cases where surgery could be the last resort. Any damage unnecessarily damage done by the knife, can not be undone.

Eternal truths are ever fated
To be persistently restated.

From the Little Book of Pithy Verses. Editor

Chapter 41 – PERSISTENT OFFENDERS

Hospitals and prisons have a lot in common. Each provides a range of secondary benefits for those inmates, who already have the primary "benefit" of a psycho-neurosis.

Of course there are plenty of people, who contract organic illnesses, or are unfortunate enough to have accidents, but that category of patient would not fill the hospitals. If it were not for those who are in hospital on account of a psycho-somatic illness caused by a psycho-neurosis, or who are hypochondriacs on account of a their psycho-neurosis, the hospitals would not be overcrowded.

Prima facie, such victims of psycho-neuroses should want to be liberated from the psychic problem which holds them in thrall, but there is the problem of their secondary benefits. Only the hypochondriacs and the sufferers from psycho-somatic illnesses can judge, whether the secondary benefits from their condition make their dependence on the medical services worthwhile for them. Only they can tell whether they want to be healed.

Similarly, there are people who are brought up to be thieves, or who become criminals by force of circumstance, but if it were not for those who get involved in criminal behaviour through the influence of their psycho-neuroses, the prison population would be much smaller. Like some patients in hospitals, some criminals in prison see prison as their way of life. But for those secondary benefits, all such prisoners should want to be rid of their psycho-neuroses. The secondary benefits figuratively hold the prisoners in fetters preventing catharsis, however much they ought to want to get out of prison.

Unfortunately, those prisoners do not choose to lose their liberty, any more than habitual gamblers choose to lose their money. It is not "their" decision. In the context of compulsions and obsession, it is "not their fault". In one sense, they can not help themselves.

That fact does not serve as an excuse for their crimes. You have to apply the test of whether they would have committed those crimes if a policeman were standing at their elbow. For the people, who are habitual criminals from the affect of psycho-neuroses, the answer is "No". If a policeman were standing at their elbow they would not do it. They know what they are doing, and that what they are doing is wrong. Just as the psycho-neurotic glutton still puts the food into his mouth while thinking of his diet, so the recidivist criminal commits another crime, while wishing he was doing something else.

The pious wish, that they had been doing something else, does not come to their aid when standing in court awaiting the verdict of the jury. They are guilty, and they must be deterred by one means or another from committing other offences. Unfortunately, neither punishment nor preaching can overcome the affect of their psycho-neuroses. It is one thing, to establish that you are perfectly sane and reasonable in making your decisions, while there is a relevant "policeman" at your elbow, but it is quite another to resist the contradictory force of your psycho-neurosis throughout the public daylight hours in public, and the lonely watches of the night

Sometime, somewhere, in the twenty-four hour days of the seven day week, the urges and cravings of a psycho-neurosis are liable to break through the barriers of reason, and cause people to do, what they do not really want to do. Every obese dieter, who pops another bite of something into his mouth, is well aware of that truth. Every nail biter, searching for another bit of nail to bite, knows it too.

Those people, who are called "habitual" criminals, but who are really criminals on account of a traumatically acquired psycho-neurosis, can be regarded as unfortunate. On the other hand, they do have the same "advantage" as the people tossing and turning in their beds. They have plenty of time and opportunity in their seclusion to meditate in search of their own traumatic memories. They can then discharge the affect of their psycho-neuroses, the affect of their emotional constipation, by overt physical reaction like crying, screaming, speaking or simply repeated blowing. They need not hold back. They have no need to be embarrassed, because screams in prison are nothing unusual, and the disturbance is well worthwhile, provided that the scream is directed to the discharge of the blocked emotion attached to the old traumatic experience.

Habitual criminals have another advantage in this matter. It is an advantage they have even over sleepless people tossing and turning in their beds. They can ask the government to provide them with hypno-analysts.

****

Needs must where the devil drives
Proverb

That devil, like the daemons, which drive some
people to suicide, are often just psychoneuroses.
Editor

****

Chapter 42 - KALEIDOSCOPE

The variety of affects, which can be produced by the loose innervation from a repressed experience is infinite. In consequence they cannot be corralled into a list. All one can do, is to demonstrate the diversity of potential affects.

The fact that the body can be affected by a thought in the mind is clearly illustrated by a simple blush. Your mind has an embarrassing thought, and the body responds by sending a rush of blood to the arteries in the face. Similarly, extreme fear in the mind can affect the gut. That truth can then be clearly seen in the pants. It shows that involuntary muscles can be affected by psycho-neurosis, as much as voluntary muscles. In the same way, the mind can paralyse individual voluntary muscles or of whole limbs.

Another possible affect is that the endocrine system can be thrown into disarray, because a thought which produces anger or fear, can also produce the discharge of a hormone to galvanise you for fight or flight. In that way a mechanism as delicate as the fertility cycle, can be arrested, or thrown out of kilter. Any mixed set of symptoms can be produced, so that any known organic illness can seem to be imitated. Stress, depression (whether relatively casual or so called clinical), anorexia (or conversely bulimia) dyslexia, way-out fantasies, apparent past life regressions or simple nail biting, you name it, and if it has no other identifiable cause, it is probably due to a psycho-neurosis. In other words, it is caused by emotional constipation.

Psycho-neurosis can take the form of paranoia, or it may produce a phobia. There is a list of phobias in this book, but even that long list can not claim to be complete. Psycho-neurosis can take the form of an aversion to anything. Conversely there may be an obsession, and there is no way in which all the conceivable obsessions or compulsions could be listed.

So much for affects causing afflictions, which have been given a name. Listing the way in which, and the degree to which, likes and dislikes, attitudes and moods, prejudices and predilections are formed is quite impossible. They would, of course, seem to be part of the individual's personality. They are what make those individuals the persons who they are. The question is, whether those people are boorish, mawkish or vociferous of their own free will, or whether a psycho-neurosis is pulling the strings? If those people knew what is shaping their behaviour, their moods and their attitudes, would they choose to stay like that, or would they prefer to have their supposedly "free will" set free of their psycho-neuroses ?

The point is that the choice is not theirs. As long as they have such psycho-neuroses they are their slaves. Their intellect may tell them that they want to do something, but they "can not bring themselves" to do it. It feels as if they were attached to a piece of elastic, which does not quite stretch. That piece of elastic, moreover, is as strong as a steel cable.

Conversely, people may ask themselves: "Why do I keep on doing something which I do not want to do. Why do I keep eating, when I want to slim?" or "Why do I keep smoking when I want to stop?" The answer is always the same. It is an inaccessible traumatic experience which prevents free association of ideas from taking the logical path from the problem to the solution.

Claustrophobia, to the point of homelessness, agoraphobia, hypochondria, sleeplessness or inability to relax, attitudes or inhibitions, inability to socialise, whether incapacitated or whether driven, the kaleidoscope of psycho-neuroses provides an infinite variety of aspects.

Just as a kaleidoscope provides the fascination of a myriad of patterns by means of the single operating method of shuffling a few bits of coloured glass, so the kaleidoscope of psycho-neurosis only has a single cause, namely emotional constipation. The mechanism is always the same, and there is only one solution. That solution is the discharge of the repressed emotion, which is causing the problem.

Finally, it should not be supposed, that trauma is a prerequisite in the kaleidoscope of psycho-neuroses. Pleasure can be encapsulated in a psycho-neurosis just as much as a painful experience, if the pleasure is perceived in a state of pleasant surprise, or high excitement amounting to a hypnoid state. That fact is illustrated by the case of a man, who found himself unable to walk past any shoe shop without stopping to gaze at the display of feminine footwear. In hypnosis he recalled an incident in his infancy involving his nursemaid. Wheeling his pram in the park on a hot summer's day, she took off a shoe, and used its tip to tickle is winkle. He had evidently found that pleasurable, and was just as much in fetters to that pleasurable psycho-neurosis as people are to traumatic psycho-neuroses. In that way, pleasures experienced in a hypnoid state, may be the root cause of personal fetishism. Very often premature sexual experience is the traumatic cause of psycho-neurosis.

****

"A man, who is forever disturbed about the condition of humanity, either has no problems of his own, or has refused to face them."
                    Henry Miller - Playwrite

****

Chapter 43 - RESEARCH

The existence of psycho-neuroses, including psycho-somatic illnesses, is generally accepted by the public, but that acceptance is based on anecdotal evidence. The Studies on Hysteria contain five major examples of that type of anecdotal evidence, and this booklet contains five more. Every day, hundreds of therapists and thousands of patients proceed on the basis of such evidence, but sceptics demand scientific "proof".

What the sceptics want is measurement and repeatability. That does present some difficulties, because many illnesses are not amenable to measurement, and secondly, no two patients are alike. Thirdly, once a psychoneurosis has been resolved, it has gone, and the cure can not be repeated. Even in the case of Bertha Pappenheim the exact cure could not be repeated, because every one of her sequence of neuroses was different. Fortunately she had the unhappy knack of giving herself a new neurosis, as soon as the previous one was cleared up. That enabled Josef Breuer to assure himself that the cures, which he had witnessed, were not just coincidence. They were cause and effect. (Where the cause is the discharge of the affect, and the effect is the cure.) Latter day researchers do not usually have access to such convenient cases.

Despite those difficulties, the scientific method could be invoked in the study of psycho-somatic afflictions, because some afflictions can be measured over an extended period of time. Sperm count is an excellent example, and the resulting counts could be plotted against time. If the affliction continues, the graph should provide an almost horizontal, straight line, or display minor ups and downs. Either way, the patient's condition would be a matter of clinical record.

At some time during the period of those counts, the patient could take part in hypno-analysis. The period of that analysis could be recorded on the graph. If the graph showed a discontinuity in the form of a permanent rise in the sperm count, precisely after the hypnotherapist had reported catharsis, that medical record would provide significant evidence. One such medical record by itself, would prove nothing, but if the same discontinuity were found in a significantly greater number of cases after analysis, than is found in a control sample without hypno-analysis (i.e. a sample which did not involve psycho-therapy) the inference must be, that the therapy caused the discontinuity in the graph, by resolving the psycho-neurosis which had caused the low sperm count. Even if a discontinuity in the graph were to show up during, or some time after, the conclusion of analysis, it would provide information calling for further investigation

Some sceptics might raise objections on the grounds that the discontinuity was not found mechanically every time there has been successful therapy (i.e.therapy leading to visible catharsis). That would be a misunderstanding of the scientific method. Gravimetric analysis is a very accurate method of determining the weight of a substance in a chemical sample, but it is not expected to give the exact answer every time.

THEORETICAL SPERM COUNT GRAPH

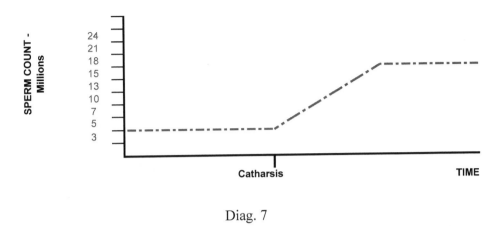

Diag. 7

Theoretical spermcount graph as it might look before and after therapy has produced catl
Good semen should contain something between 15 and 20 million sperm per milliliter.
Let us say 5,000,000 before catharsis and 17.500,000 after catharsis
The point of catharsis should be indicated jusr before the discontinuity.

The result of the weighing might be vitiated by experimental error or sampling error. Therefore chemists do the same analysis two or more times, in the hope that two results will be identical. It may be that an analysis has to be done several or even many times, as was the case in the problem of discovering atomic weights. In such cases, those results which are identical (while others are scattered around) are taken to be the correct result. The same certainty would be achieved by scrutiny of a significant number of graphs.

Such a method of clinical research, independent of the opinion of the consultant, the therapist and the patient can be employed in connection with any illness, which has a measurable symptom. Diabetes, leukaemia and focal length of the lenses of the eye are just random examples of what could be scientifically investigated in that manner. The proportion of cases, in which hypno-analysis is followed by a discontinuity in the graph would, no doubt, vary from syndrome to syndrome, depending on how frequently psycho-neurosis imitates that particular organic affliction.

As always in science, a negative result is as valuable as a positive one. The research may prove that there is no psychological component in the illness under investigation. In any event, all research into the presence or absence of a psycho-neurotic affect in a clinical syndrome can at present only be carried out by means of hypno-analysis.

Chapter 44 - PARTING SHOT

All psycho-neuoses are a flight from reality. Although they produce an infinite variety of results, they all involve the same mechanism. Hence, despite the immense diversity of their affect, this book inevitably involves frequent repetition. There is no reason why this parting shot should be any different to the preceding chapters in that respect.

This book is not about psycho-therapy in general, nor about hypno-analysis techniques in particular. It merely draws attention to the existence of the phenomenon called psycho-neurosis, and to the effect which the existence of such an afflictions (affect) has on individuals, and on society.

Nevertheless, I do not want to leave you to face the unwelcome memories you may have in a tranquil moment at a lonely bus stop during the day, or in bed during the dark watches of the night, without any means of confronting those echoes of the past.

We all have some more or less disagreeable incidents in our lives. It is not always possible to react to those incidents, as immediately or as fully, as would have been appropriate. The emotion from such incidents, experienced in an emotionally inconvenient moment, can have been choked back, and thus resulted in emotional constipation.

If you recall a disagreeable event, and merely turn it over in your mind, it will just go back into the subconscious mind, from whence it came. Any affect, which unbeknown to you it has had on you, will remain.

If, on the other hand, you verbalise, if you vocalise, if you say out loud, what you think or feel about that event, you may get surprising insight into that experience. You may find that it affected you more deeply than you had realised. If you then give any consequent physical reaction like tears, tremors or speech, free rein, the emotional hang-up (which that reaction has disclosed) will be discharged. In consequence, any affect which that hang-up had on you, in terms of health or behaviour, will disappear. Such vocalisation of your experience is not a case of "talking to yourself". You can talk to the wind rustling through the trees in the day time, or talk to the ceiling above your bed at night. Either way your subconscious mind will be unburdened, and you will: "have got it off your chest".

Finally, and by no means least, if you read through the list of common expressions at the end of Chapter 22, you may recognise the instantaneous hypnoid state, which came upon you in the course of some "long forgotten" untoward incident. If you then give verbal expression to the feelings you had in connection with that event at that time, you may experience the relief of catharsis, and the **"surprising, liberating enlightenment"** which comes with it.

POSTSCRIPT

That brings me to the reason why I have written this book. The aim of the book is surprising, liberating enlightenment. You may have found this book surprising. You may even have found it enlightening, but the enlightenment from reading this book is nothing compared to the enlightenment you will get, when free association in (self)hypnosis guides you to the site of your own traumatic memory. Until then, you may be surprised by what you have read, and enlightened by what you have understood, but you will not be liberated.

Every psycho-neurosis is a flight from reality. The consequences of that flight can not be predicted. Neither can those consequences be overcome by willpower. They can be overcome by giving way. If a door will not open outwards, pushing against it will not achieve your aim. However much willpower you exert, however hard you push on it, that door will not open outwards. I have written this book, because I would like everyone to know, that if a door will not open outwards, you must open it inwards.

If you keep pushing against a door, which will not open outwards, in order to keep reality at bay, you are turning yourself into a prisoner. That door simply will not open outwards. You must open it inwards, and let reality come in. Once you come face to face with the unseen monster behind the door, it will dissolve into thin air. Then you can move out of your prison into a new life, surprised, enlightened and liberated.

The liberation comes when you relive your traumatic experience, and make an overt physical response to the recollection of that fearful event. To achieve that liberating moment, let go of your resistance. You must face up to the everyday reality from which you once fled. Then, the psycho-neurosis, which you did not know you had, will be gone.

Shakespeare summed up that paradox when he said: "There are more things in heaven and earth than are dreamt of in your philosophy". Because you have read this book you know how right Shakespeare was, when he wrote that phrase. Now that you are privy to this secret, other people will never seem the same again.

Recollection without affect almost invariably produces no result.
Preliminary communication to the Studies on Hysteria
Breuer & Freud

95

DICTIONARY

In this book the terms listed below are intended to have the following meanings:-

ABREACTION is the name given to the process involved, when a traumatic experience is recalled, and the long delayed emotional discharge takes place.

AFFECT means, either the feelings (emotion) to which an experience gives rise, or the psycho-somatic illness, psychic disturbance, behavioural disorder or immune system damage, which you suffer instead of the emotion. In this book it is intended to mean the latter. (See also Effect)

BLOCK is a colloquial word for a psychoneurosis resulting from a trauma.

BREUER'S METHOD, also known as the Talking Cure, is to put the patient into hypnosis, let them find the problem in his or her subconscious mind, and recount the causative event to discharge a psycho-neurosis

CATHARSIS means purging. It takes place, when (for whatever) reason a repressed memory is recalled, and the affect, to which it gave rise in lieu of the relevant emotion, is discharged.

DEFENCE is the sequence of events which sets in, when fear of an emotional overload drives an experience out of the conscious mind into the subconscious.

EFFECT means the direct consequence of a cause. The effect of a punch on the nose is, that the broken blood vessels bleed. The affect is that it makes you angry. (See also Affect).

EGO is the Latin word for I. In hypno-therapy it means the essential YOU, the way you think about yourself as an individual.

EXTERNALISATION means attempts to transfer affect of an experience into action on the outside world.

HANG-UP is a colloquial word for psycho-neuroses resulting from a trauma.

INNERVATION means the nerve signals arising from the repression of a traumatic memory, which keep the substitute affect of the repressed trauma in existence.

MEDITATION means a hypnoid state in which resistance is overcome and traumas can be recalled.

PSYCHO-NEUROSIS is the condition in which loose innervation from a repressed traumatic memory produces an unpredictable affect.

REPRESS means suppressing a memory to the point, where resistance sets in to prevent its recall.

REPRESSION means the action of suppressing a memory so effectively, that it is locked into the subconscious mind, and can not normally be remembered in the waking state. Some therapist reserve that term for sexual traumas.

RESISTANCE is the subconscious process, which operates to keep a memory hidden, after a traumatic idea, thought or experience has been hidden in the subconscious mind by defence.

SECONDARY BENEFIT The primary benefit from a psycho-neurosis is that the individual did not and does not need to suffer the relevant emotion which has so far been avoided. The secondary benefit is any advantage, which accrues to the patient from having the psycho-neurosis (e.g. Disability benefit).

SELF-PUNISHMENT means harmful behaviour, which is due to the undischarged affect of a traumatic experience

SUBCONSCIOUS in this book means the subconscious part of the mind. It is the part of the mind, which is, so to speak out of sight, and is to that extent at a "lower" level than the conscious mind, but it is working for you all the time. It works for you when you are awake, when you are asleep, and even when you are unconscious. The subconscious is sometimes spoken of as the "unconscious". (but see unconscious)

TOTALITY OF STRESS means the total stress arising from the sum of different nervous excitations.

TRAUMA means a wound or injury, including an unbearable experience, which is psychologically injurious.

TRAUMATIC means something, which is (psychologically) injurious

UNCONSCIOUS is the word to describe the condition you lapse into when you have been hit over the head with a log of wood. Unconsciousness takes place when the conscious mind, and a part of the subconscious mind, is disabled. Unconscious has drifted into use to describe the subconscious, because the early texts on hypno-analysis and psycho-therapy were all written in German. In that language the subconscious processes are said to be "unbewußt" i.e. not aware, whereas the unconscious is spoken of as "Bewußtlosigkeit" i.e. Consciouslessness. Early translators of the German texts were not psychologists, and so stumbled into the error of translating "UNbewußt" as UNconscious.

WILLPOWER in this book means the psychological force used to produce denial or dissociation, by means of which a traumatic experience is locked into a hypnoid state.

INDEX

Distant Memories

You drag around, without a doubt,
hang-ups, which you could do without.
They weigh you down, and sadder still,
they fetter, what should be free will.

In deep recesses of your mind,
there lurks a thought you can not find.
It visits you from time to time,
but it is not, what it might seem.

Though it would go against the grain,
it would still be a worthwhile gain,
if you could peer into the past,
and come to terms with it at last.

It seems a distant memory,
But, it is not just history.
You must recall it, and relieve
your erstwhile anger, shame or grief.

But yet again, it might be guilt,
on which neurosis has been built.
If guilt is found, and then removed,
your whole condition is improved.

To find the thought that plagues you so,
hark back to days of long ago,
when things weren't what they are today.
Your fetters would then fall away.

So, do not long procrastinate.
Just find out how to meditate.
Identify your inner strife,
and thereby get yourself a life,
but if your trouble still persists,
consult an hypno-analyst.

Peter Breuer

CATHARSIS PAGE

Note of Bad Memories revisited
(Hang-ups Discharged)

Make a list of experiences, in which you have now discovered, and duly felt previously unrecognized emotions.   -   Use this space.

A REVEALING INSIGHT INTO
THE SUBCONSCIOUS MIND

EVERYONE A WINNER

COCKTAILS:- "Shaken, not stirred"   *007*
EMOTIONS:- "Stirred, not shaken"   *Editor*

A HOLLANDER PUBLICATION

E-mail: hollanderpublications@hotmail.co.uk
    or: hollanderbooks@gmail.com